The Complete Guide to
Windsurfing

The Complete Guide to
Windsurfing

Jeremy Evans

Facts On File Publications
New York

Contents

The Complete Guide to Windsurfing
was conceived, edited and designed
by Holland & Clark Limited

Photographer
Alastair Black

Additional photographs were supplied
by the following: Chelsea Wharf
Windsurfing, Jeremy Evans, Fanatic,
Hayling Windsurfing, Andrew Hooper,
Klepper, Roger Lean-Vercoe, Mistral,
Christian Petit, Neil Pryde, Sodim,
Tabur, Cliff Webb, Alex Williams

Designer
Julian Holland

Editor
Philip Clark

Artist
Nicholas Hall

Assistant Editor
Gill Clack

Design Assistants
Martin Smillie
Stephanie Todd

The Complete Guide to Windsurfing*

Published in the United States of America
by Facts On File, Inc.,
460 Park Avenue South, New York, N.Y. 10016.
Published in Great Britain by
Bell & Hyman Limited, London

ISBN 0-8160-1527-9

*Windsurfer® and Windsurfing® are
registered trademarks of Windsurfing
International of Marina Del Rey, Calif.

Printed and bound in Portugal
by Printer Portuguesa
Mem Martins – Sintra

Part One

Part Two

Windsurfing for Beginners

How did windsurfing begin, and how has it developed during its first 20 years?

What are the different types of boards, and how do you tell which one to buy?

What is the basic theory behind windsurfing, and how do you learn to master the initial stages?

When the wind starts blowing a little harder, how do you handle it; and when you get into trouble how do you look after yourself?

These and many other questions are answered in the following pages.

Basic Windsurfing Glossary

THE BOARD
Nose
Front end, or bow.
Tail
Back end.
Fin
Also called skeg, to keep the board sailing straight.
Daggerboard
Large fin mid-way, which is removable from the daggerboard case. Prevents the board going sideways. A fully retracting daggerboard makes the board easier to control in strong winds.
Shims
Friction pads to ensure the daggerboard fits tightly in its case.
Mast foot track
Sliding track just forward of the daggerboard case.
Towing eye
In the nose of the board. To take a towing line.

THE RIG (moving upwards)
Mast foot
Fits into the track or mast foot well, and is normally permanently attached to the universal joint which allows the rig to be swung through 360 degrees and inclined through a minimum of 180 degrees. The mast foot/universal joint is the adaptor between the rig and the board.
Downhaul line
Attaches the *tack* (bottom corner) of the sail to the mast foot.
Wishbone
The boom, made from two elliptical alloy tubes with plastic end fittings.
Inhaul line
Attaches the wishbone to the mast.
Outhaul line
To pull the *clew* (outer corner) of the sail out to the end of the wishbone.
Uphaul rope
To pull the rig up out of the water. Attached to the mast foot by the shockcord.
Battens
Pieces of flexible fibreglass used to support the *roach* of the sail – the area outside an imaginary straight line drawn between the clew and the top of the sail (*head*). The camber is the amount of curve in the sail – ie the area between an imaginary straight line drawn from the clew to the mast, and the sail. The camber determines whether the sail is trimmed full or flat.

TYPES OF BOARD
Allround-funboard
The allround-funboard shown opposite is the most popular windsurfer for general use. It combines the stability of the allrounder, with the strong wind capabilities of the funboard.
Funboards
These tend to be shorter (less than 3.20m) and are for experienced sailors in strong winds of Force 4+.
Racing Boards
These range from boards specifically designed to race round an Olympic triangle (Open Class Division II) to funboards and allrounders.

SAILING TERMS
GENERAL
Starboard
Right (looking forward).
Port
Left (looking forward).
Windward
The side the wind is blowing from.
Leeward
The side the wind is blowing to.

POINTS OF SAILING
Leeway
Making leeway – the amount the board moves sideways, or to leeward.
Close hauled
Sailing as close to the wind as possible.
Reaching
Sailing with the wind on the beam – ie with the wind at or near 90 degrees to the board's course.
Running
Sailing with the wind directly, or almost directly behind.

ALTERING COURSE
Bearing off
Sailing away from the wind.
Heading up
Sailing up towards the wind.
Tacking
Altering course so the nose of the board passes through the eye of the wind.
Gybing
Altering course so the tail passes through the eye of the wind.
Luffing
Letting out the sail, or heading up so that the wind strikes the leeward side of the sail and causes it to lift or *back* (flutter).

WEATHER AND SEA CONDITIONS
Beaufort Scale
Measurement of wind speed based on knots – nautical miles per hour. A nautical mile equals about 1.85 km.
Apparent Wind
The wind that is experienced by the sailor – different in direction and speed from the True Wind experienced by a stationary observer.
Offshore Wind
Wind blowing on to the shore.
Tide
Coastal movement of the sea induced by pull of the sun and moon. Tide rip is when it runs extremely fast round a headland or in a confined area.

RACING
One-design
A class of identical boards racing together.
Open Class
The generic term for International Division I (stable flatboards) and Division II (unstable roundboards) racing. The standard course for these boards is the Olympic triangle which is used for dinghy competition.
Funboards
Funboards have competitions in stronger winds which are divided into course racing for the long boards; and slalom and wave performance for the shorter boards.
Club racing
Local club racing can involve any of the above categories. It may range from the very serious to a casual get together with 'anything goes'.
National Series
Racing for various national series is staged at different venues throughout the season. In the UK it may be organized by the RYA, UKBSA, BFA, Windsurfer Class, Mistral Class, etc.
International Series
There are World and European Championships for the major one-designs; and for Division II which is also the Olympic class.
Marathon
A long distance race of at least 20 miles.
Freestyle
Light wind tricks routine, usually over a three minute period.

The elements of a windsurfer are common to most marques and models, particularly if they are of the allround-funboard type illustrated here. You may find slight general differences in specification and design, and more marked differences with parts such as the daggerboard, fin, and mast foot, but once you can recognize the parts on one board you will be able to recognize them on any board.

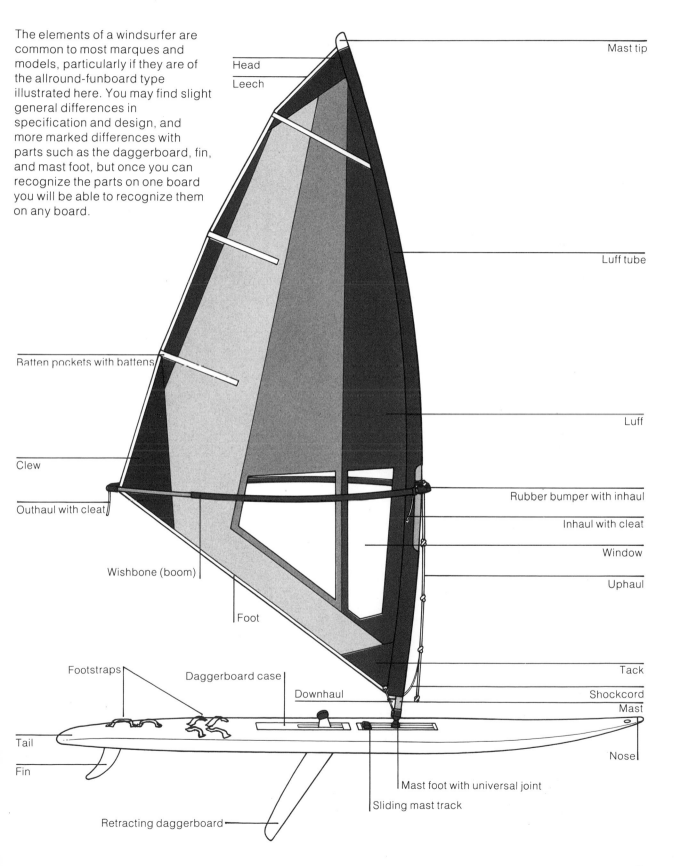

Head
Leech
Mast tip
Luff tube
Batten pockets with battens
Luff
Clew
Outhaul with cleat
Rubber bumper with inhaul
Inhaul with cleat
Window
Uphaul
Wishbone (boom)
Foot
Footstraps
Daggerboard case
Downhaul
Tack
Shockcord
Mast
Tail
Nose
Fin
Mast foot with universal joint
Sliding mast track
Retracting daggerboard

The Background

In just over a decade windsurfing has become one of the most successful new sports of the century. From a couple of people experimenting with surfboards in California, it has turned into a multi-million dollar industry enjoyed by Americans, Europeans, Asians and Australians. Its success was recognized by its inclusion in the 1984 Olympic Games in Los Angeles, which Stephan van den Berg won.

Windsurfing can be enjoyed in any place where there is sufficient water – be it open sea or a tiny lake – and in most weather conditions. True it's most fun when you do it somewhere warm with a fair wind, but so long as the ice is thin enough to break, enthusiasts will even windsurf right through a Scandinavian winter. A fair wind means the wind that suits you best, and this may mean anything from a light breeze to a howling Force 6.

Given the right equipment, there are few days when a windsurfer can't go out – no wind at all is a far more likely reason than too much of it.

There is no doubt that from the point of view of physical fitness, it is young people who take to windsurfing with the greatest ease. The peak age for top racers is late teens to a maximum of 25, after which they go downhill rapidly! However, the same is true of tennis and snow ski-ing, and with the right equipment a grandfather or an eight-year-old can still have plenty of fun.

Nor should cost be a problem. You can buy a good new board for a few hundred dollars or pounds in most countries, and if you can't afford that, there are plenty around secondhand.

Of course, you can spend a lot more on your board or boards (a real enthusiast will probably own three or four) and the same goes for the incidental costs. Unless you're lucky enough to live in the tropics, you will need a neoprene wetsuit to keep warm, and you may wish to add boots, harness, and a dry suit to the list.

Lastly, you'll need to transport the board, and unless you live right by the water's edge, that means a car with a roof rack. However, it's not always necessary to buy one. You can always share the roof space of a fellow enthusiast.

Learning

All beginners feel incredibly stupid when first having a go at windsurfing. Falling off every five seconds, they swear it's the most difficult thing they've ever done, and if that's when they give up, they carry on believing it.

However, it's not. With proper tuition (see pages 32–35) there are very few people who are incapable of windsurfing – about as many as are incapable of riding a bicycle. A two week holiday in the sun is enough time for anyone to get reasonably proficient, and in that time, those who have a good sense of balance and are reasonably fit, should be well on the way to handling stronger winds.

Advanced Techniques

Windsurfing doesn't stop when you can sail without falling off the boards.

A variety of conditions and types of boards give the sport almost unlimited possibilities. Apart from boards for general use, there are boards for racing, and boards for strong winds and waves with a variety of rigs (more cost!) These are constantly being developed and uprated, and demand board handling techniques that must improve by the day.

Most people are happy enough to restrict windsurfing to their family holidays and occasional weekends, but for those who aspire to world class regatta sailing, or jumping the waves off Hawaii, the sport must become the main reason for their existence.

Left: This is how we all start! Undignified, but easier if the water is warm (Guadeloupe here), and lots of fun to come.

Right: Windsurfing into the sunset with a nice breeze at the end of a hot day. Nothing could be better therapy after work in the office – if you're near the water.

Hoyle Schweitzer

The first published account of windsurfing occurred in August 1965. The American magazine *Popular Science* ran a feature on a 'sailboard' designed by a Mr Newman Darby ...'A Sport So New That Fewer Than 10 People Have Yet Mastered It'. You would hardly recognize it as a board today. The shape was primitive, and the square-rigger type of sail set it well apart from the board that actually caught on.

This prototype was developed by two Californians – Hoyle Schweitzer and Jim Drake. The latter was an aeronautical engineer who hit on the idea of an articulated rig. This led in turn to the universal-joint mast foot system that is used on the Windsurfer and its derivatives today – Windsurfer with a capital *W* is the brand name of board that resulted from the work of these two men: *windsurfing* or *boardsailing* is the generic name for sailing it.

On 26 April 1969 Drake presented a paper at a technical symposium on sailboat design, entitled *Windsurfing – A New Concept In Sailing*. It revealed that he and

Left: A jovial Jim Drake on the beach in Hawaii, looking at developments in the Pan Am Cup. Although with no commercial interest in windsurfing, he still shows up at regattas.

In the early days of board development, he experimented with a mast rigidly attached to the daggerboard which could only move fore and aft – his articulated universal joint represented the vital breakthrough.

Above: Hoyle Schweitzer sitting on a pile of cases containing his Windsurfers (for the 1980 World Championship in the Bahamas). He developed the hot moulded polyethylene method of construction for the board, which has been used by his Licensees in the Netherlands (the biggest), Japan, and Australia. All Hoyle's family windsurf – his eldest son Matt has long been rated one of the best in the world.

Schweitzer had tried out a number of designs. A year later Schweitzer had them in limited production.

The Windsurfer

The Windsurfer was the first board to go into production, but with Schweitzer's limited financial resources it was the Europeans who paved the way for the sport's present-day popularity.

The large Dutch 'textile manufacturer Ten Cate heard of the Windsurfer in 1970, and sent representatives to see Schweitzer with the idea of selling him sailcloth. That deal was never completed, but they came back with 100 of his boards. The following year the quantity was upped to 1000, and 3000 the one after. The US production couldn't keep up with this demand, so armed with a licence to manufacture, Ten Cate set up their own factory in Holland, retaining their licence until 1984.

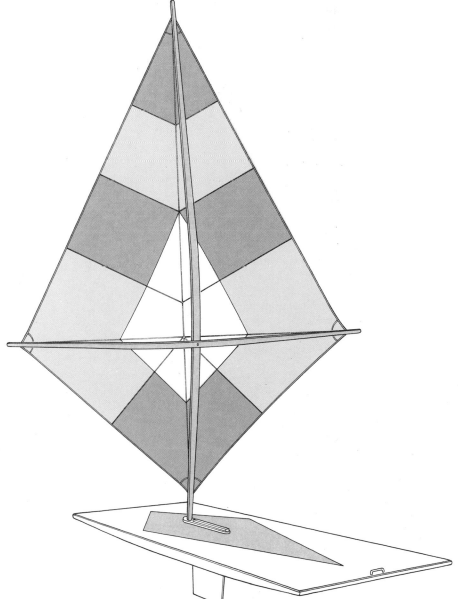

Right: Newman Darby's board had a very different rig. The early windsurfer prototypes looked fairly primitive, but one cannot imagine this rig ever being as efficient upwind. It has been resurrected in recent years to prove 'prior art' in the legal proceedings concerning Schweitzer's Patent in Germany, and the UK with Peter Chilvers'. It never had any great commercial success, and Newman Darby lives quietly in the USA.

The Patent

In 1968 Hoyle Schweitzer and Jim Drake filed an application for a Patent to cover their invention in the USA.

Shortly afterwards Hoyle bought out full interest in the project to go it alone, and also filed his Patent in the countries where he thought his Windsurfer would be most successful – the UK, West Germany, Australia, Japan and Canada – he had to be selective as he couldn't afford to apply to every country in the world.

Since that time, the success of windsurfing, which has led to it being copied worldwide, has also led to considerable legal wranglings for Hoyle Schweitzer. He has never been able to exercise any control over what goes on in the 'un-patented territories', notably France, but where his Patent holds sway he has granted licences to produce boards built and designed by other manufacturers.

In return for their licences, these companies agreed to pay Schweitzer a royalty of approximately 7.5 per cent on every board. Not surprisingly, several other major manufacturers were unwilling to pay this amount, or in some cases were unable to get a licence agreement.

Their boards flooded the German market putting the licensed boards at a disadvantage, but after long-drawn-out court cases German Law upheld the Patent in 1980.

The same problems were deliberated over in British courts and the

The original Patent document that started it all. Patent litigation has tended to rest on the wishbone and universal joint. On the whole, the Patent issue has been successfully overcome, with compromise on both sides.

PATENT SPECIFICATION (11) 1 258 317

1 258 317

DRAWINGS ATTACHED

(21) Application No. 10919/69 (22) Filed 28 Feb. 1969
(31) Convention Application No.
716 547 (32) Filed 27 March 1968 in
(33) United States of America (US)
(45) Complete Specification published 30 Dec. 1971
(51) International Classification B 63 h 9/08
(52) Index at acceptance
B7V 72 73
B7B 244 423

(54) WIND-PROPELLED VEHICLE

(71) We, HENRY HOYLE SCHWEITZER AND JAMES ROBERT DRAKE of 317 Beirut, Pacific Palisades, California, United States of America and 385 Mesa Road, Santa Monica, California, United States of America respectively; both citizens of the United States of America do hereby declare the invention, for which we pray that a patent may be granted to us, and the method by which it is to be performed, to be particularly described in and by the following statement: —

The field of art to which the invention pertains includes the field of ships, particularly sailboats and iceboats, and the field of land vehicles with sail propulsion.

Sail propulsion has been suggested as a motive means not only for boats and iceboats, but also for such watercraft as surfboards and landcraft such as sleds, i.e. generally any lightweight small craft. Typically, a sail is provided on a mast that is rigidly secured to the craft in a vertical position and additionally described the sail and mast can be enjoined in a network of riggings and control mechanisms.

The general effect of providing a sail on a normally sailfree vehicle is to convert the vehicle into a water or land-boat. Thus, by rigidly securing a sail to a surfboard, the feel of the surfboard and enjoyment as such is lost and the skill normally required to control it is no longer needed. Instead one obtains the speed and feels of a light sailboat and needs substantially only those skills appropriate to control a sailboat. The same "denatur..." occurs with other vehicles modifi... ... ...ear a sail.

A problem a... ...n a sail is fitted to a vehicle that ... ...have high roll stability in that ... ...xcessive winds can overturn th...

A need there... ...safely providing wind-pro... ...e vehicle not normally so... ...means

preserves the original ride and control characteristics of the vehicle.

In accordance with the present invention there is provided a wind-propelled vehicle comprising body means, an unstayed spar 50 connected to said body means through a joint which will provide universal-type movement of the spar in the absence of support thereof by a user of the vehicle, a 55 sail attached along one edge thereof to the spar, and a pair of arcuate booms, first ends of the booms being connected together and laterally connected on said spar, second ends of the booms being connected together 60 and having means thereon connected to the sail such that said sail is held taut between the booms.

In particular embodiments, the spar is connected to the vehicle body by means of 65 a universal joint, i.e. a joint having three axes of rotation.

The pair of arcuate booms are provided laterally disposed on the spar to hold the sail taut and provide a hand hold for the 70 user.

The invention can be used on watercraft, iceboats and landcraft. It can be used on small yachts, runabouts, canoes, rowboats, and other such craft, but is most 75 advantageously used on small and lightweight vehicles such as surfboards, iceboats, and sleds. Leeboards can be provided for a watercraft of low roll stability such as a surfboard. The term "leeboard" 80 used in the specification and claims is meant to include center boards and dagger-boards, as these terms are known to the sailing art, as well as other projections from the body of the craft, planar or otherwise extending 85 into or onto the water for stabilization.

The present invention allows essentially all of the steering and control to be accomplished through the sail; i.e. no rudder or other steering mechanism is needed, although such need not be excluded. One may 90

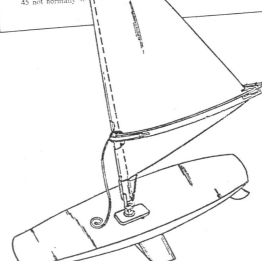

net result in both countries was a certain amount of compromise on both sides. Many manufacturers agreed to honour his royalty terms, and Schweitzer took a far easier line on granting licences to those who required them.

Apart from a dedicated minority of windsurfing 'superstars', the USA remained largely uninterested in windsurfing until the early 1980s. Then, having swamped their own countries, the European manufacturers began an onslaught across the Atlantic, with extensive Patent litigation resulting once again – which was doubly acrimonious with the first windsurfing Olympics being held in Los Angeles.

European Manufacturers

Once the Windsurfer began to catch on in Europe, rival manufacturers were not slow to join in the new craze.

Windglider was started by German entrepreneur Fred Ostermann in 1975, followed by the Swiss Mistral company in 1976. Hi Fly, Sailboard (both German), and Bic (French) followed, and these became the major manufacturers. Between them they swamped the two biggest markets – Germany and France – with a total of over 250,000 boards by 1982, before transferring their interests to the USA which suddenly opened up as the virgin land of windsurfing. The UK remains a poor relation with maximum board sales of around 30,000.

Besides these big mass-volume manufacturers, there are hundreds and probably thousands of other companies producing boards – some with the capacity for several thousand units per year, others just turning out custom made boards at the rate of two or three per month. In Europe there may be 200 or more manufacturers, and Far Eastern countries are busy turning out replicas of European boards.

As one of the world's largest windsurfer manufacturers, the Swiss Mistral company remained unlicensed until 1981, when due to the Patent action in the German courts they had to pay large amounts of back royalties. Schweitzer subsequently eased up considerably on his policy of granting licences.

Windsurfing Today

From Schweitzer's first boards, windsurfing has evolved rapidly in a variety of directions – in some cases it has turned back full circle to being a surfboard with a sail!

However, for most people a sailboard is something for occasional use. They haven't the time or the inclination to get involved with the more rarified aspects of sport, and the great mass of the market is, and always will be, served by the general purpose board that every major manufacturer has within its range.

Bic, Hi Fly, Alpha, Mistral, Vinta and all the other well known brands produce at least one board which is flat, stable, and around 3.60m in length. Their price and performance are closely allied, and in many cases it is only the striping on their hulls, or the company's aggressive marketing policy, that sets them apart.

The Next Stage
Once bitten, some want to progress a little further than enjoyment on the occasional weekend. They can either turn to racing, or to a style of sailing which is orientated to mastering stronger winds.

Racing
A windsurfer performs as well as any dinghy, and racing and regattas are now a popular part of the windsurfing scene.

You can go racing in the evenings after work, travel across the country for a weekend national event, or across the world for a week-long international championship.

The most popular marques have their own one-design events, while most other flatboards are suitable for beginners' racing. The more experienced sailors will turn to funboard events for strong winds, or Division II triangle racing for lighter winds.

In the early 1980s the Division II 'roundboards' were considered the Grand Prix league of windsurfing.

Above: Taking off near Diamond Head, Hawaii. Few windsurfers have the ability to sail like this, but many aspire to it.

However they are unstable to sail and extremely specialized – and also tend to be rather expensive! The consequence is that their popularity has waned, and many prefer to sail funboards.

Stronger Winds
As their techniques improve, sailors find that they can master stronger winds. At the same time the necessary windsurfing equipment is being improved all the time.

For most people, the best boards for strong winds are funboards. They are easy to control, and with the addition of design details such as footstraps, and special daggerboards, skegs, and rigs, are marketed solely for sailing in winds of Force 4+.

All the developments in this part of the market have been led by the highly romanticized sailors of Hawaii, immortalized in thousands of colour photos, leaping skywards from the waves, and sailing strong winds is now very popular.

The Record Breakers
The types of boards available have multiplied rapidly, and so have the variety of disciplines within the sport.

There are now special strong wind regattas where you can't race if the wind is less than Force 4; wave jumping competitions where the sailors are judged on style and achievements; and speed trials where boards sail timed runs through a 500 metre course in the hope of breaking a world record.

In the past few years, boards have sailed round Cape Horn (Frederic Beauchêne); across the Pacific and the Bering Straits between America and Russia (Baron Arnaud de Rosnay); around Great Britain (Tim Batstone); and across the Atlantic (Christian Marty and Frederic Giraldi). It is a tribute to their organization and common sense that the number of fatalities and casualties generally has remained small.

Escalating Costs
As the disciplines within the sport have grown, so has the cost. It's no problem if you stick with your learner's board, but one day you may find you need: an allround-funboard for general use; a Division II board for triangle racing; and a short funboard for strong winds. You will also need a variety of sails and accessories to go with them, and in a highly commercial business you will find that when you are racing you are up against professionals.

Windsurfing has become far more professional than sailing. All the major manufacturers pay top sailors to help market their products, and there are now an increasing number of events with cash prizes – the sailors get out what they put in.

Right: Just what many of us want! The short board is fun, but needs a lot of experience to be safe.

Types of Boards

The five boards on these pages cover most aspects of the sport.

A professional might well have one of each, and a great many more besides. He would also be changing and updating them at least once a season. More than likely he would be supported by a manufacturer, otherwise he would have to spend a great deal of money.

Most of these boards are turned out on production lines by the major manufacturers, though the very specialized ones are often hand built. For instance, a wave jumping board currently being shaped in Hawaii won't be in full stream production with a major manufacturer for at least another six months, and then will rapidly be outdated by another new shape.

However, whether or not a board is of the most up-to-the-minute design is largely irrelevant to all but the most enthusiastic and advanced sailors. The major manufacturers offer a well-presented product which is simply a variation of that offered by their competitors. Every now and again one manufacturer gains a temporary advantage, but construction and marketing techniques are so sophisticated that there really is little to choose between the different products.

One should also remember that the five categories of boards represented here overlap. The course racing funboard is a specialized version of the more humble allround-funboard, while the latter may only be a modified version of the basic flatboard. The short board may range from a buoyant 3.20m down to a 2.60m sinker, and there are many variations in between. Unfortunately no one type of board is suitable for everything, and most enthusiasts will have at least two boards.

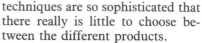

Basic Flatboard
The type of board that started it all, the best to start on, and the most popular for allround use. Flat, stable, and forgiving, almost every manufacturer has a board like this in his range.

Normal dimensions are: around 380 cm long; weighing about 19 kg; with a sail between 5 and 6.5 sq m. Material could be polyethylene, ABS, or fibreglass. Typical examples are made by Bic, Wayler, Vinta, etc, and many feature the option of uprating their specification.

Allround-Funboard
This has displaced the basic flatboard as the most popular type you will see today. Sizes and shapes are much the same, but the allround-funboard comes with all the trimmings of footstraps, small retracting dagger, and mast track. None of these details will help the learner; but they are a bonus when you move on to stronger winds since they make control of the board easier. Price normally reflects specifications.

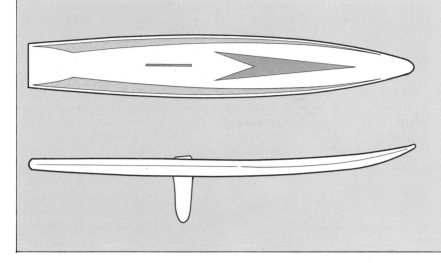

Open Class Division II

The Open Class roundboard was considered the Grand Prix racing board with the most advanced design characteristics. These boards are for triangle racing only – they are tricky to sail owing to their rounded shape, and tricky to manufacture down to minimum weight due to their high volume which may exceed 300 litres. Some are hollow with a foam sandwich skin, while others are 'custom made' from a foam block.

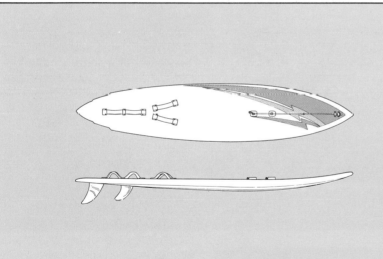

Funboard

The true funboard is designed for use in Force 4+ and must be planing all the time. The longest boards of this type are around 3.20 m and may have a small daggerboard, but a length of around 2.90 m is far more usual, giving the right mix of speed and manoeuvrability while being relatively easy to sail. Most of these boards are 'marginals' which can be uphauled, though the specialist technique of waterstarts is preferable.

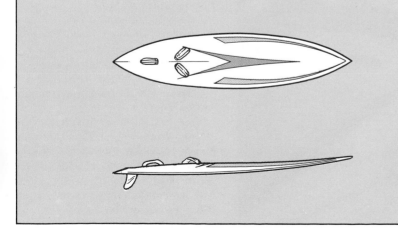

Sinker

The extreme surfboard for real experts evolved in Hawaii in 1981. Very short (say 260 cm), light (8 kg maximum) and with minimal buoyancy (waterstarts and high speed power gybes are mandatory) boards like this are invariably built one-off. Simply a shaped foam block covered in glassfibre or something like Kevlar, it will have one to three skegs and footstraps, with the mast foot located forward.

One-Designs

A one-design is a class where all the boards are the same, and can therefore race on equal terms with no advantage in equipment deciding the winner.

The most obvious example is the Windsurfer, which is still almost certainly the most numerous marque in the world, but in order to keep pace with the times its specification has had to be changed. Early models featured teak booms and plywood daggerboards which would make the board uncompetitive today, but the spirit and basic principles of the class have remained the same.

Other one-designs tend to come and go according to their popularity in the market. While the Windglider was the Olympic board it remained popular, but as soon as it was replaced it virtually disappeared from view. The old style Mistral Competition was produced in at least four guises and was the mainstay of Mistral World and European Championships before being dropped from the range in 1986. It is still raced keenly on a

Above: Windsurfer one-designs racing at close quarters in their World Championships (Bahamas).

Left: Mistral Competition – a one-design which has proved particularly popular in the UK.

national basis in countries such as the UK, and for this specific purpose secondhand models are much sought after.

For those who are keen on racing, a one-design offers safety in numbers which guarantees enjoyment and makes it a safe investment. The wellbeing of the class will depend on the enthusiasm of the members who work for the Class Association, plus the help of

The 1984 Olympic Windglider sailing downwind in difficult conditions – or perhaps the driver just wanted a rest. Controversy surrounded the choice of this board as the first to take part in an Olympic regatta.

any financial contribution from the manufacturer or importer of the board.

For a small membership fee a member can expect: 1. A regular monthly newsletter containing information on events. 2. A chance to advertize secondhand equipment. 3. The offer of an advantageous insurance deal. 4. Regular regattas, on a local or national basis. 5. Class association get-togethers – perhaps a film show in the winter. 6. The chance to qualify for international regattas, with costs paid by a sponsor.

Also, the most popular one-designs are able to offer: local racing on summer evenings and weekends; weekend national events; and week long European and World Championships.

All the racing tends to be based on the Olympic triangle where possible, though with reasonably short legs so that races in a fair wind last well under an hour. A typical weekend or week long event will have five or six identical races with an Olympic scoring system deciding the eventual winners.

Only with a very small entry will there be a single winner, as most of the one-design classes are divided into 'weight groups'. Given the same ability, a lighter sailor will travel faster than a heavier one, particularly when the board lacks buoyancy and is pushed down into the water by weight. So, to prevent the lightweights winning every race, Windsurfer class racing, for

instance, is divided into a total of five groups with five overall separate placings. The sailors are weighed before the event and are divided into: light; light-medium; medium-heavy; and heavy – plus a separate group for ladies. (Other classes may only have two weight groups).

There is seldom an overall winner of the triangle racing, but these events also tend to feature several other types of competition, and sometimes have an overall 'pentathlon' winner.

The 'freestyle' is a three-minute routine for the sailor to show off his tricks on the board. A very rarefied skill, it has become so competitive that some sailors specialize in this alone.

'Slalom' is a knock-out competition for two boards on a short slalom course, depending on skill in quick tacking and gybing.

The 'Long Distance Race' is, as its name implies, a race of considerable length (anything up to 25 miles), frequently with a Le Mans style 'beach start' and long reaching legs.

The Olympics

In 1980 the IYRU chose the Windglider as the first board to race in the 1984 Olympics in Los Angeles. Unfortunately the choice had political overtones. Even though the Windsurfer had more widespread support and popularity worldwide, the Windglider was the only likely contender being built behind the Iron Curtain (in Hungary).

For 1988 the IYRU made a less contentious choice by opting for Division II for the Olympic Games in Korea.

Open Class

The IYRU Open Class Division 2 rules are set out in detail in the Glossary at the end of the book. In brief they require a board of maximum length (390 cm); minimum weight (18 kg); and maximum depth (22 cm) – though this ruling was only introduced after the European Championship in 1980.

The Boards

These rules are surprisingly tight and have led to look-alike roundboards since the Tornado first appeared, and won the European Championship in 1979.

Designers discovered that the key to speed was a very buoyant board with the least possible wetted area, which would plane long before a flatboard on any point of sailing. Once they caught on to this principle, they made even thicker boards, so that some boards at the European Championship of 1980 were deeper than they were wide – with the result that they were very difficult to sail, and hopeless in strong winds.

The 22 cm maximum depth measurement resulted, and now it is difficult to tell the hull shape of one roundboard from another.

Events

Division II racing is always round an Olympic triangle, with a separate class for the women and two weight groups for the men of up to 70 kg (lightweights), and over 70 kg (heavyweights). This is because the lighter sailors will always tend to have a speed advantage.

Since the early halcyon days the popularity of Division II as the leading development class has waned, but there is still a highly enthusiastic minority who race these boards. The class is most strongly supported in France, while the UK, Holland, Sweden, Germany and the USA have also held major championships.

You will seldom see a Division II board in a windsurfing shop. They are produced in small numbers by a handful of manufacturers, and the problems of producing a high volume board (the maximum is about 325 litres) which is both stiff and light means that prices are inevitably at least $1,200 for the board without the rig.

The rigs are very different from those seen on most allround-funboards. They have a triangular outline with a very long boom of around 2.70 m, and the rules are so stringent that the sail shape is virtually standard with an area of approximately 6.3 sq m.

The choice of Division II as the Olympic board for 1988 has given the class a big lift. It remains the fastest type of windsurfer in winds up to Force 4, and is almost certainly faster than any other sailing craft round an Olympic triangle.

Division I

In 1980 the IYRU introduced the idea of a new Division I for flatboards. They reasoned that since these were the boards that the great majority of sailors owned, there should be a class to cater for them.

The rules were in essence the same as Division II, except for a maximum hull depth of 16.5 cm so that the boards would be flat and stable. The three International One-designs – Windsurfer, Windglider and Mistral Competition – were automatically included, but the class soon ran into trouble when it was found that few production boards would actually measure to the rules. In 1984 the Division I rules were therefore updated, but it remains a class which has never proved universally popular.

Left: Open Class racing with Karl Messmer (Mistral M1) to windward of two Windglider Mach 1's and a French Crit. Messmer won the Open Class World title three times before transferring his interests to jumping waves in Hawaii.

Right: Surprisingly little has changed since the early days of Division II. This photo was taken at the European Championship held in Yugoslavia in 1979, and immediately afterwards the rules which still form the basis for the class came into effect. More modern hulls are a little rounder and deeper; while sails are less wrinkled!

The Professionals

Despite overlooking the fact that a great many 'amateurs' are very obviously professionals, the IYRU and various national authorities (such as the RYA in the UK) take a firm stand over the question of advertising.

Advertising contravenes their Rule 26, for racers are not allowed to wear a sponsor's logo on their clothing or sails, and the boards themselves can only have their brand names in the very smallest lettering.

However, the sport has reached the stage where many of these undeclared professionals have got used to making a very good living from it, and, with their sponsors, they welcomed the creation of a professional World Cup circuit in 1983.

The World Cup is the most important annual pro series, with six or more events held at locations in various parts of the world. Top names in the series are sponsored by board manufacturers, sailmakers, and other windsurfing interests; and if they're lucky they will get additional income from outside the sport – Audi, Carlsberg, Swatch, Jantzen and Penthouse have all added to the incomes of leading racers in recent years.

The income of a windsurfing professional is not in the same league as some other sports, but it can still be substantial. Robby Naish is the world's most successful racer and best known pro ever, and his annual income exceeded $100,000 by early 1980. Other pros now have earnings in the same league, and worldwide the number of professionals estimated to earn a good living out of the sport is around 40 men and 10 women, while many others earn just enough to support an enjoyable lifestyle.

There are now big professional events in most countries that give substantial cash prizes to the winners. Most windsurfing competition has bypassed the IYRU and national sailing authorities, and the only possible drawback for a top sailor being a windsurfing professional is that he cannot take part in the Olympic Games.

Speed Sailing

The RYA first organized 'Speed Trials' in England in the early 1970s. They chose the enclosed Portland Harbour near Weymouth on the South Coast, running their event for one week each year in October, when in theory the wind should blow hardest.

The aim of these trials is to be the fastest sailing craft over a timed run of 500 metres – they set a circle of buoys with a 500 metre diameter which the craft can enter at any angle, so long as they pass the

The first British professional event was the Bacardi Isle of Man World Cup, held in 1981.

correct side of a centre buoy and go the full distance.

This event was never intended for boards, but by 1980 they were dominating it. In 1977 Derk Thijs had sailed a standard, but very light Windglider to 17.1 knots, and in 1979 Clive Colenso raised this to 19.2, sailing an Olympic Gold in 40 knots of wind.

By this time other countries were organizing their own Speed Trials, in part due to frustration with the Weymouth weather. Hoyle Schweitzer set up his own *Maalaea Speed Trials* on the Hawaiian island of Maui in 1980, allowing the Dutchman Jaap van der Rest to push the record to 24.45 knots.

From there on the record has repeatedly been broken, with Speed Trials held at Portland, as well as in France, Holland and Australia.

The Boards

In 1981 the West German Jürgen Honsheid ran at 24.75 knots on a surfboard with a windsurfer rig. From there on all serious speed sailors have used the surfboard style sinker, which has the least resistance to going fast in the really strong winds necessary to break a record.

With the use of sinkers and improved rigs speeds have crept up, with Fred Haywood (USA) first to break the 30 knots barrier in 1983. By 1985 the record stood at over 60 kph, and for many years boards have been the fastest sailing craft in the world – only the British proa *Crossbow* which ran at 36.04 knots in Weymouth back in 1980 has gone faster, and it is only a matter of time before a board overtakes it.

The type of board which has proved fastest for speed sailing since it was first pioneered in 1981. Length is usually around 2.50 m, with a scant 60 litres of volume.

Wave Jumping

Wave jumping got started on the simple premise that if you sail fast at a wave which is also coming fast towards you, you will take off.

If the board is light and your technique is good, you will do so consistently, a fact first hit upon by the Hawaiian windsurfers who did so much to popularize and romanticize this aspect of the sport.

The great originators were Larry Stanley and Mike Horgan, who hit on the idea of a harness to reduce the strain on your arms, and footstraps to keep you and the board together.

By 1978 they had convinced Hoyle Schweitzer that he should produce a strong wind version of the Windsurfer. The resulting board was called the Rocket. They moved the daggerboard well and mast foot aft; put two skegs in place of one; gave the bow some more rocker for the waves; and bolted on footstraps.

The Rocket was the first production wave jumping board. The Hawaiians continued to lead the way with development, building one-off custom prototypes for their own use, which were snapped up by Europeans eager to try the Hawaiian experience. The most successful Hawaiians could sell their expertise to the European volume manufacturers who were clamouring to add boards suitable for wave jumping, riding, and general strong wind use to their ranges. Rick Naish, Brian Hinde, and Ed Angulo are among those who have designed for the world market.

Why Hawaii?
Wave boards are totally unrestricted by rules, and the Hawaiian weather (hopefully, though not always) provides constant Trade Winds of Force 4 and more in a balmy climate, which means that the sailors can try out new boards, equipment, and techniques every day. The Pacific waves come in on a 1000 mile reach, breaking on the coral heads to provide ideal waves – altogether the conditions can never be bettered in Europe, which experiences both cold winters and far less predictable wind patterns.

Therefore the Hawaiians will remain at the forefront of strong wind board development, and Europeans who feel frustrated by this fact simply solve the problem by going out and joining them.

Developments
The design and construction requirements of strong wind boards are similar, whether the boards are for wave jumping, wave riding, speed sailing, or slalom style racing. Conditions are rough, so the boards and their rigs must be easy to handle, and robust enough to withstand speed and waves.

Since the Windsurfer Rocket, boards used for fun in strong winds have become shorter, simpler and lighter.

At first much of the emphasis was on jumping, but it was soon realized that any board that is small and light will easily get airborne. From there on development has concentrated on waveriding abilities and general strong wind control, and for the expert this is widely regarded as the ultimate form of windsurfing. Rather than tacking, a wave board has to be power gybed, being kept permanently on the plane to prevent it from sinking beneath the sailor's weight, which puts it rather beyond the ability of the average (or even well above average) windsurfer.

Wave jumping has become a highly sophisticated performing art! There are wave competitions, and the very best sailors are capable of looping the loop.

The Big Events

Most big events are designed around strong winds when windsurfing is at its most challenging and exciting. Waves are an added bonus, and the locations with the most reliable conditions feature annual regattas which always attract the top sailors.

Hawaii is at the top of everyone's list. The combination of Trade Winds and big Pacific rollers have made this the classic venue for all wave events. On the main island of Oahu the most important location is Diamond Head, while on the nearby smaller island of Maui, Hookipa Beach Park is famed for its challenging conditions.

There are four or five international wave events in Hawaii each year, during which competitors sail in a 'man-on-man' knock-out competition. The sailors are awarded points for their prowess on the waves with the winner going through to the next round; the marking system can be most closely compared to a freestyle ice-skating competition.

Other countries that have the right conditions for the big wave events are Australia and South Africa, with the months either side of Christmas being favoured for the best windsurfing. In Europe the waves are not so consistent or so big, but there is still plenty of wind for funboard racing.

Force 4 Plus

A minimum wind speed rule is common to all funboard racing, but apart from that almost anything goes and it is frequently used as a prototype testing and development ground by the manufacturers.

This is particularly true of the World Cup circuit, which is windsurfing's version of the Formula 1 Grand Prix Championship. All the sailors are entered by 'works teams' consisting of board manufacturers and sailmakers; and if you go to watch a race meeting you will find them all in their own enclosures with designers and racers conferring on ways to go faster.

Virtually all the boards are custom made prototypes, and if they're successful they invariably appear as the next year's production boards. They are either 'course racers', which are high performance allround-funboards of about 3.60 m; or 'slalom' boards which are much smaller (about 2.70 m) and designed primarily for speed on a simple course in and out through the surf which can be the most difficult conditions.

Venues for the World Cup change from year to year. The most popular are Nijima in Japan; San Francisco in the USA (where they race beneath the Golden Gate Bridge); La Torche on the northwest Atlantic coast of France; and Sylt (W. Germany) and Scheveningen (Holland) on the North Sea.

Anywhere Warm . . .

When not engaged in the World Cup, the top sailors have a dozen other major events to choose from in the international calendar.

Apart from Hawaii the warm waters of the Pacific host the Guam Cup; while equally benevolent conditions can be found in the Caribbean which is best known for the Hang-in and Hook-on, a two week annual cruise throughout the Virgin Islands with racing for production and prototype classes. Anyone can enter, with a fleet of yachts following the boards and stops each night.

Robby Naish in waveriding action at Hookipa. Robby is Hawaiian born (1963) and bred, and first started winning at the age of 13. Since then he has won almost every big event in the windsurfing calendar.

Tandems

Every windsurfer should try a tandem at least once. They're great fun, and it makes a real change to have someone else on the board enjoying themselves with you.

It used to be claimed that they were also faster than one-man boards. This is certainly no longer the case as they are far too heavy, but they make up for it with an impression of speed.

Production Tandems

A limited number of manufacturers have tandems in production. Well known marques have included Windglider, Shark, and Rainbow, but due to disadvantages of weight, price and storage the concept has never had any more than limited popularity.

Most tandems have a large single daggerboard with a big fin at the tail. They have mastfoot positions at front and back for two sailors, and usually have a central position so the board can be sailed with one rig singlehanded.

In fact due to their size and stability they make excellent platforms for learning, and some schools use them for personal tuition with the instructor at one end and the pupil at the other.

The old fashioned tandems such as the Windglider were very long (6.5m) and very heavy (60 kg). More recent designs such as the Rainbow are 'funboard tandems' which are considerably shorter and more sprightly; and special one-off custom tandems have become part of the scene at the major speed trials. They are not quite as fast as the singlehanded sinkers, but still manage to clock respectable times at over 25 knots!

Racing Tandems

In lighter winds tandems are faster than conventional boards, and Open Class Division III is the IYRU's two-up racing version of Division II.

The boards have the same rounded hulls and triangular-shape rigs, but are twice the length. Racing tends to be confined to a few enthusiasts, with an annual championship on Lake Garda.

Technique

First of all, you need to decide who is captain, and sail as a team. The forward sailor backwinds the aft sailor, so he must take care not to sheet in too tight or the aft sailor will fall in. Sailing upwind, the aft sailor will sheet to the centreline with his rig raked forward, while the forward sailor sails with his rig more free, and rakes it a little aft – the Centre of Effort is somewhere between the two.

On the reach, the aft sailor will always heel his rig more than his companion – you'll have to work out whether the board goes faster with the lighter or heavier sailor in the forward position.

When running you can goose-wing with one rig on either side, making the tandem particularly efficient on this point of sailing.

The procedure for tacking is started by the aft sailor and completed by the forward sailor – when gybing it's the other way around.

Some of the speed tandems are sinkers, and with them the technique is very different. They need to be water started since there's not enough flotation to carry the weight of the sailors at low speeds.

Turning is virtually impossible. The board is too small to be tacked and there's not enough room between the rigs for the sailors to gybe. The only answer is to fall off, swim the board round until it's facing the opposite direction, and waterstart to get going once again.

Right: Three-up! This 'tridem' was seen at Weymouth Speed Week.

Starting Windsurfing

There are numerous clubs and class associations you can join once you become involved in windsurfing. Whether you want to race, or simply exchange information and possibly equipment, there are organizations run by enthusiasts and professionals on a local or national basis.

Getting Started
You will benefit from joining one of these organizations before you have even stepped on a board. They will be able to provide the information on where and how to learn, and what equipment to buy. If you haven't already learnt the basics through hiring a board on the beach, or being coached by a friend, they will also be able to advise you on taking a course with a properly trained instructor.

Teaching Courses
Unless you have a genius's ability to pick up the sport, a proper teaching course will save you a lot of wasted time, and implant good techniques for your future sailing.

It is wise to go to a properly recognized school, which in most cases will be sanctioned by your national sailing authority (see Glossary). For instance, in the UK the Royal Yachting Association (RYA) is the national sailing authority with its own Boardsailing Committee, which runs a teaching scheme for windsurfers based on IWS guidelines.

IWS
International Windsurfer Schools were founded by Dagobart Benz, a former member of the German Olympic Star team. He evolved a structured teaching system which has been the foundation of the sport's success in Europe.

First steps on a Windsurfer. A small sail, not too much wind, and a warm climate make all the difference when getting started.

Benz owned a hotel in Germany, on Lake Constance, and having mastered windsurfing himself in the very early days, realized that his guests would need proper instruction to get the same enjoyment.

He therefore developed a step-by-step system of teaching, and went on to set up IWS schools all over Europe – you can recognize them by their orange flag with a black Windsurfer logo.

He trained supervising instructors to ensure that exactly the same format was followed, using the same syllabus and issuing the same certificates. They then went back to their own countries to instruct yet more instructors, enabling the pyramid to grow and grow.

Having qualified as basic instructors, the next step was for them to gain practical teaching experience, before returning to attend a re-assessment course leading to a full instructor's licence. This re-assessment remains, and serves the dual purpose of keeping instructors up-to-date with the latest teaching techniques and maintaining high standards in the schools – principals are required to hold a full licence which must be reapplied for and renewed every two years.

Other Courses
The IWS system ensures worldwide high quality teaching, and is either followed verbatim or adapted by the relevant national authorities in all windsurfing countries.

For instance, in the UK, the RYA takes it that much further. They require an instructor to do the following: pass his instructor's course; pass an open sea test designed to ensure competent board handling in open sea conditions; hold a valid first aid certificate.

Like the IWS, RYA schools must: have a qualified instructor; provide wetsuits and buoyancy aids for their pupils; have proper changing and teaching facilities; and have a powered rescue craft on hand.

Duration
An IWS course is designed to last a full day of around eight hours. Many beginners find it easier to spread this over two or three sessions, and the schools are normally willing to make allowances.

If the weather is unsuitable (generally too much wind), you can expect to be asked back on another day at no extra charge. The overall cost will of course reflect the facilities on offer – some will be notably more luxurious and comprehensive than others.

Necessary Equipment
The school provides the board: it also provides the wetsuits (though you won't need these if you are lucky enough to be learning in the tropics).

It is up to you to find out if they provide food and refreshment or accommodation. You should normally expect to take your own towel, bathing costume, and a pair of soft rubber-soled shoes. Bare feet may grip well enough on a board, but at first you will probably find shoes are better, and that they help to protect your feet.

Format of a Course
The order and timing of a course will depend on the instructor's personal preference, coupled with weather and tidal considerations.

The order of the items may vary, but you should always expect to come across the following:
1. Introduction and simulator
You may have paid a deposit, the full amount, or you may be expected to pay on arrival.

You then get shown around and introduced to your fellow pupils (never more than eight per instructor – the fewer the better), before running through the basic parts of a sailboard, and being introduced to the dry land simulator.

This is a board mounted on a pivoted turntable (or more often the central section of an old board that has come to the end of its life afloat).

It enables you to learn the basic techniques of windsurfing without moving from a fixed spot, and without falling in and getting wet. This technique greatly cuts down teaching time, as you are not being blown away from your instructor, and are not preoccupied by being cold and wet.

You are shown how to get on the board, which will be less stable than one on the water; how to raise the rig ready for sailing; how to turn the board, sail it, steer it, and tack and gybe.

The instructor will demonstrate all these manoeuvres, and then each member of the class will be required to run through them, noting and learning by one another's mistakes.

Finally, having finished with the simulator, you will be shown how to assemble and stow the rig, as well as very important self-help techniques.

2. Tethered boards

The idea of being on a tethered board is that you can get your balance, pull the rig out of the water, and attempt to get going without being blown away by the wind or swept off by the tide – your board is tied to an anchor like a dog on a leash.

The movements you practise will be the same as those on the simulator, but the difference is that you will be falling into the water every few seconds.

Unless you are exceptionally hardy, this makes it worth ensuring that you choose a time of year when the weather is reasonably warm. This will be a far greater worry than feeling silly when you can't stay on the board – the great thing about learning in a class is that everyone else experiences exactly the same problems.

3. Group sailing

After the tethered board you can try sailing off untethered, and it's immensely rewarding when you first sail along for half a minute without falling in – every windsurfer remembers this first achievement.

As well as sailing in a straight line, you must get back to where you came from. You will have to steer the board, turn it round, and then sail it upwind, until you can sail a small triangle by the end of the course.

Weather permitting this should be possible, and so long as you don't get cold or exhausted (the two are synonymous) intervals between falls should get longer and longer.

4. Theory and detailed rigging

This is a vital part of the course, even if it takes considerably less

The simulator can be little more than a plank of wood on a turntable, with a windsurfer rig.

Alternatively it can be a full board, but either way it is as difficult as standing on a board in choppy water. The difference is that when you fall off you don't get wet and cold, and spend minutes getting back on – you simply step down on to the ground.

The pupils practise pulling up the rig, turning the board beneath the feet, and simulate sailing. Each one is criticized, but there's no need to get embarrassed – you learn from each other's mistakes. After the simulator you can get out on the water where conditions are likely to be very different. The simulator is used throughout the world – by any school that uses an IWS based teaching system.

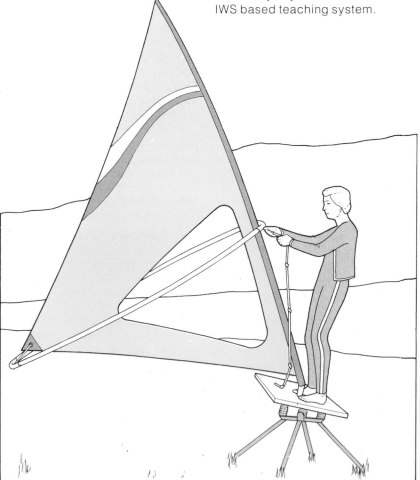

time than practice on a simulator or afloat.

Most newcomers to windsurfing have no experience of the sea and its behaviour, and they must learn the basic laws of safety, seamanship, and courtesy afloat. Even experienced yachtsmen have to learn to tell the differences – for what is safety to them may be danger to a windsurfer.

Finally, the theory of why a sailboard does what it does must be mastered before you can control your board properly.

5. Final assessment
The instructor will decide whether you have accomplished enough to

be issued with a basic certificate of competence – in some countries you are required to present this before you can hire a board or take to the water.

The majority will pass first time, and depending on the school there may be some questions on theory or a sailing trial, but nothing very onerous. Those that don't pass can come back for a further session.

Results
By the end of an IWS based course you should be able to sail a board in light winds where you choose with a small rig. You should know how to rig it and pack it all up, and you

Many simply learn by watching a friend on the beach, but a proper teaching course will probably teach better techniques.

should have the necessary knowledge to make the sport a safe one.

Going it Alone
If you're a lone wolf and would rather go it alone, you can teach yourself to windsurf to a basic proficiency standard from the section in this book between pages 52 and 75.

After that, stronger wind sailing and the more advanced techniques follow.

Buying a Board

The sport of windsurfing has grown so rapidly that for the manufacturers it has become like the fashion industry. Each year they introduce new models and complete new ranges, and though these may be partly justified by developments in design and manufacture, they will owe more to the strategies of the marketing men who want to keep their particular company in the forefront.

This is both good and bad when it comes to buying a board. On the one hand it guarantees that there will always be plenty of excellent buys available secondhand; on the other, if you want the latest and most up-to-the-minute creation, you must take care that it won't lose most of its value as soon as it's superseded by the next development.

The Major Marques
The ranges of most of the major manufacturers cover the five categories of boards listed on pages 18 and 19:
1. The basic flatboard
2. The allround-funboard
3. The Open Class roundboard
4. The short funboard
5. The extreme strong wind sinker

The first-time buyer should always consider the first two categories as the ones to go for. Within them there is a vast choice, and he is unlikely to make a bad buy so long as he sticks to a well known brand of board.

Basic flatboards are also readily available secondhand. The Windsurfer Regatta or Mistral Competition, for instance, are first time buyers' boards par excellence – they have been established for years, continue to be very good to sail, have enthusiastic one-design followings, and are consequently widely sought after.

If you're buying new the most popular choice is an allround-funboard which can be used for progressing to handling stronger winds. If it's fitted with footstraps leave them off while you're learning (they just get in the way); and if there's a sliding mast track set it in a fixed central position.

Remember that the major manufacturers compete directly on price and quality, and cannot afford to get the construction or design of a board wrong when they are tooling up for minimum runs of thousands of units. Even if they do change models each season, the new ones are developed from successions of prototypes which guarantee that the end products are reliable.

Price Differentials
The world market is dominated by a handful of manufacturers from Germany, France and the Netherlands.

Ninety per cent of their market is made up by the flatboard, allround-funboard, or shorter funboard, and since they are all producing a very similar product there is scant allowance for variation in price.

Some boards are very cheap, while others aim to have the kudos of being the best. For instance, a board from Mistral may be twice the price of a board from Bic. Its equipment and performance may be marginally superior, but it has the 'name' to sell at a far higher price, and continue to hold that price in the secondhand market. It's all a matter of status!

Boards and Rigs
Most boards are sold complete with rig. However, rigs are interchangeable from board to board, and when you progress to owning three or more boards, you will begin to buy rigs and boards separately.

For the first-time buyer it is best to stick with the rig recommended by the manufacturer. This will seldom be the height of sophistication, but when you don't have the experience to tell the difference, it hardly matters.

You will probably have the option of different sail sizes. Again, which one you choose doesn't matter much in the long term. As you progress through the sport you will find that you need at least three different sails to cope with varying wind conditions.

The illustrations on pages 80–81 show a typical range offered by a sailmaker. An average beginner wants a sail that is easy to handle; say 4.8 square metres for someone who is relatively small; 5.6 sq m for someone of average strength; and a full 6.5 sq m for a six footer who is fit and young.

Choose which sail suits your physical capabilities best when starting to windsurf; then add more sails as you improve your technique.

Ancillaries
Getting equipped for windsurfing can involve spending a lot of money. You will need:

A car – unless you can borrow one. (A Suzuki jeep has just the right image.)

A roof rack – if this doesn't have a lock, it may be worth investing in a board lock to prevent your windsurfer being stolen.

Insurance – against the board being stolen, unfortunately an increasingly popular pastime. This will also help pay for broken masts and boards.

A wetsuit

Boots

Gloves

A dry suit – *de rigueur* in cold water.

A harness

You will of course also need the *board* (or boards), and a *rig* (or rigs) with several *sails*. Thankfully you won't have to buy the whole lot at

Despite its racey appearance, a light beginner could learn on an allround-funboard like this (3.35 m). Heavier beginners will need a bigger board with more volume for stability at low speeds.

once, and you can always save money by borrowing equipment, or buying some of it secondhand.

Other needs include *spare parts* (the mast foot breaks every now and then), *tools* (at least a knife and a screwdriver), a *repair kit*, various bits of *spare line*, and possibly some *certificates*.

The necessity for the certificates varies from country to country, and from place to place. To hire a board, race it, or just to take your own on a certain piece of water may require an official-looking piece of paper. Enquire before you go – your national sailing authority may be a good source of information, and if you need a certificate for sailing abroad it can usually be provided for a modest fee.

In other circumstances you may have to prove your worth, and a RYA Certificate given to those who successfully pass their learners' course is fairly useful.

The Elements
The board
Made from plastic, there should be no bumps, hollows, or cracks. The join along the sides should appear perfect. There should be a good non-slip finish on deck, but be wary of hard angles – odd-shaped decks tend to be cosmetic rather than functional.

The hull should be completely foam filled. Check that there is enough buoyancy to carry your weight – at least 180 litres for 10 stone.
The fin
Plastic – 'Lexan' polycarbonate or stronger glass-filled polycarbonate.
The daggerboard
Plastic, and for ease of use retracting completely into the hull. You occasionally find alloy or laminated plywood daggerboards on race boards – they are lighter and stiffer, but the ply ones require careful looking after.
Fin boxes, daggerboard cases, mast foot wells and tracks

Either integral with the moulding of the board, or separate plastic units bonded into position. Often one specialist manufacturer supplies the same units for several different boards, so they are interchangeable.
Universal joint
The rubber coupling which is variously called the 'UJ' or 'power-joint'. It links the rig to the board.
The mast
Usually glassfibre made on the same principle as fishing rods. Tapered alloy extrusions are used for racing, but are more likely to suffer damage.
The wishbone
Rubber sleeved alloy with plastic end fittings. The less flex the better.
The sail
Quality of cloth and cut vary. There are all sorts of sail materials from basic Terylene sailcloth to more fancy Mylar laminates with superior weight and stretch characteristics.

Where to Buy
A specialist dealer with a windsurfing school attached to his shop should be able to give advice, and provide a full service back-up including warranty work, repairs, replacements, and trade-ins (most dealers will now take boards in part exchange).

However you may prefer to explore the secondhand market. Either way, remember:
* *The latest in regatta or short boards may be very expensive when new. As it is superseded, its value will plummet.*
* *Better to stick with a board that is still in production and selling well.*
* *A board made from a tough material will hold its value well.*
* *Boards break up. If the foam inside a board begins to delaminate, restoration will be expensive.*
* *Check the equipment. Rigs are expensive, and there is a great difference between a good sail and one that is the wrong size and blown out.*

Most shops have a wide range of boards and accessories, and are run by staff who are enthusiasts. This normally means that their advice can be relied upon when you don't really know what to buy. Unless you are very sure of your ground, always go for a well known brand, and if possible seek advice on it. There have been few horrors from the major manufacturers in the last few years, though it's true that some boards are not quite as good as others.

Right: Racing boards tend to be very specialized, and the Division II boards shown here only account for a very small part of the market. At the top level of competition they tend to be both fragile and expensive.

Care and Repair

A board that is misused will deteriorate rapidly, particularly if the construction is fragile. If you are the sort of person who enjoys messing about doing minor repairs, well and good, but if you'd rather never lift a finger, think twice about that board with the ultra-thin gel coat.

General Upkeep

Cleaning the board
Try a proprietary domestic cleaner. If there is any tar on the board, go over it with white spirit first.
Storing the board
Boards can warp. Always store your board with support along its full length.
Sails
Roll a sail with full length battens. Alternatively 'flake' the sail with parallel folds along the luff and leach. Avoid creasing the window.

Give the sail a bath. Leave it overnight in warm water containing detergent. If there are any stains in the morning, give it a scrub, and then rinse in fresh water.

Tar can be dealt with by carbon tetrachloride or petrol, but always check colour fastness before you get carried away.

Repairs

Minor repairs to the board, such as scratches and cracks can be dealt with by the amateur. Major repairs are best left to the professional, who has the right equipment and the experience of having done the job before. It is not necessarily difficult, but on your first attempt you stand a good chance of making a mess, so if it's a new board leave it alone.

The major materials all have different properties when it comes to repairs.
Polyethylene
Can be welded using a soldering

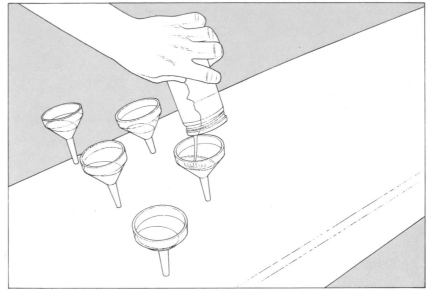

Above: The repair and modification of old polyethylene boards has become a fine art. One way of replacing soggy foam is to cut it out, patch the area over, and then pour in liquid foam.

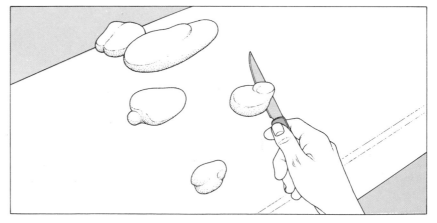

Below: The foam expands and solidifies, and the excess can be scraped off with a sharp knife. It is unlikely to be a very beautiful repair, but it should be effective and rejuvenate the board.

iron, a Stanley knife, and polyethylene rod. Cross-linked polyethylene has the reputation of being very difficult to deal with – if you're unsure leave it to a specialist who can use a proper heat welding gun.
ABS
Cracks can be filled using a solvent paste which dissolves the surrounding plastic. This can also be used for applying ABS patches.
ASA
Has a tendency to discolour when

subjected to amateur repair, and is safer left to the professional.
Glassfibre
Theoretically the easiest material to repair. Bits of missing gel coat can be re-gelled, and glass mat added for extensive repairs.
Foaming
The central core of most boards is the foam. If this needs replacing, a section can be cut out so that it can be re-foamed. This does not apply to polystyrene foam.

Major Damage

The most common breakages are masts and daggerboards. Glassfibre masts can be repaired, while daggerboards are cheap to replace.

Most board damage can be repaired. Minor skin damage is fairly easy to put right, but curing more major damage may require specialist knowledge.

Suitable materials are available with instructions which should be followed to the letter for safety and a successful result. The easiest type of repair is one with epoxy resin.

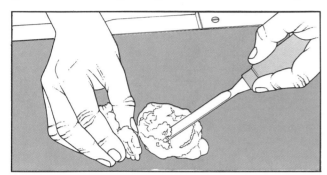

In some cases the skin and the foam below it will be damaged. Cut away the damaged skin, and then dig out the wet or damaged foam using a knife. To finish the job you will need adhesive tape, epoxy resin, glassfibre, polyurethane foam, cellulose putty, acrylic paint, and basic tools.

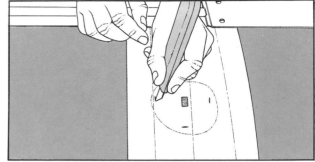

Make the hole perfect, and cover the repair area with adhesive tape. Cut a hole in the middle through which you pour the foam which is supplied as a two-part liquid. The other smaller holes are for air. Once mixed the foam expands and solidifies rapidly.

The hardened foam should be cut and sanded back level beneath the outer skin of the board. You then make an outer gel coat, using epoxy resin (the hardener) and chopped strand mat glassfibre. The masking tape is to guard the surrounding area against splashes from the resin which is highly caustic.

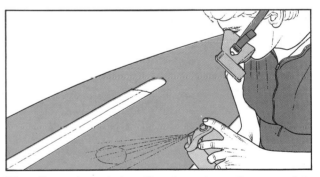

When the resin and glassfibre have 'cured' you can fair the patch down level with the outer skin of the board, using sandpaper, filler, putty and patience if you require a cosmetically perfect finish. Finally a spray gun is used to finish the repair with a matching paint or non-slip finish depending on requirements.

Fibreglass masts are very prone to damage. You normally get a clean break at the wishbone, and this can be repaired using a 'sleeve', for which you can use a section of an old mast (above). Glue it inside or outside with epoxy resin, and then wrap fibreglass tape around it.

It is possible to reinforce your mast at the base, wishbone attachment, and tip, by wrapping round fibreglass tape treated with epoxy resin. This won't affect the flexibility of the mast.

The base of the mast is liable to splinter, but it can be bound with synthetic thread.

Windsurfing Accessories

Windsurfing is big business for manufacturers and retailers. As far as they're concerned, once you get started you don't just buy a board and leave it at that.

They want you to come back and buy a short funboard and a racing board, and to keep on trading them in for newer, better models each season. They also expect you to be suitably dressed, with the flashiest of wetsuits for windsurfing, and the very minimum of a Hawaiian T-shirt for après-windsurfing.

Apart from the clothing and the boards, they would also like you to spend your money on every kind of hardware.

Is It Worth It?

You should never forget that the manufacturers and the retailers are there to make money, and you should therefore treat their products with a certain amount of caution. As with many other sports only a few items of equipment are absolutely vital.

What You Really Need

On the following pages we shall run through the items you really need, for yourself and the board.

Proper clothing is very important and should be carefully chosen. Unfortunately price does tend to reflect quality, although there are short cuts. If your budget is limited, you can make a very acceptable wetsuit from a kit, using the offcuts for neoprene socks which you can wear with oversize tennis shoes. You won't be the best dressed windsurfer, but you can still overtake him in a flurry of spray.

You could also overtake him wearing secondhand gear, for as accessories are restyled and revamped for each new season, so the trendiest windsurfers sell off their gear to keep abreast of the times. It's lucky that most clothing is made to a high standard, and will be good for several more years after a solitary season's use.

Proper accessories for your person include wetsuit, footwear, gloves, and eventually a harness. You may wish to add a buoyancy aid, and if it's cold you should also add a dry suit.

Proper accessories for your board amount to a roof rack, some straps to tie the board and rig to it, a lock, and possibly a trolley.

However if you feel you want more, there are plenty more accessories of varying usefulness.

Bags

You can get bags for your board, rig, and daggerboard.

A bag for your board is useful if the board is fragile, or perhaps you feel it might fade in the sun?

A bag for your rig is very useful. It should be a long sausage which will take a rolled-up sail plus mast-foot and all the battens; or alternatively an even longer sausage which will take the mast with the sail rolled round it (battens removed). The bag should be rainproof, and a Velcro fastened pocket on the outside is always useful.

A bag for your daggerboard is only useful if the daggerboard is very fragile – ie an expensive laminated wooden job for racing. Then it should preferably be heavily quilted.

You can also have a personal bag to carry all your odds and ends. The yachtsman's soft carry-all is recommended – the best ones have separate sections for wet clothing and pockets for tools, tape, etc.

Strong Wind Sailing

Strong wind sailing accessories are endless. Apart from half a dozen sails and three wishbones, there is:
A mast track
More expensive boards tend to have sliding mast tracks as standard, while they are optional on some cheaper boards.

Once you are proficient the sliding mast track allows you to trim the rig for optimum performance, and makes strong wind control much easier.
Footstraps
More and more new boards have the option of footstraps which can be left on or off. They're well worth considering, as once again they make the board much easier to sail in strong winds.

If the board has no provision for footstraps you can buy footstrap kits.
Fins
Fins play an important part in making boards go straight, and there are widely conflicting theories as to the best shapes and sizes. Many shorter funboards are fitted with three fins (a main fin plus 'thrusters') for extra grip and lateral resistance, and there is an endless choice in fin variations.

Unless you know exactly what you want, you will almost certainly do better to stick with the fins provided on a board. However the fin must be strong and stiff for optimum performance. It is subject to a considerable amount of side force, and if it breaks you are likely to have problems getting back to the shore.
Hawaiian uphaul
An elasticated uphaul line that has no need of shockcord to leash it to the mast foot since it's under tension all the time. Nor does it need granny knots as handholds since it's so thick and squidgy.
Mast, booms and extensions
For use in heavy surf it's worth investing in a 'heavy duty' mast. Some are guaranteed against breakage for as much as three years.

With a variety of sails you also need extensions to vary the length of the mast. These are adjustable or fixed length, as are booms which also need to be different lengths for use with different sails.

A Division II racing dagger, specially made of laminated plywood.

Clothing

You should never underestimate how debilitating cold water is, and unless you live in the tropics, you should always dress sensibly and correctly when you go windsurfing.

Wetsuit

A wetsuit is a tight fitting neoprene suit three or four mm thick. The fine layer of water between the neoprene and your body is the insulation which keeps you warm.

To work properly, the suit must be tight, but windsurfing is a strenuous sport and the suit should be flexible enough not to constrict movement. Most important of all, the sleeves should not constrict the muscles of your forearms which would lead to cramp. They should either be soft neoprene, or loose proofed nylon.

Most beginners use a 'Long John' style wetsuit. When it's cold you can also wear a wetsuit bolero top or nylon windbreaker. A

Top: A wetsuit with loose fitting sleeves does not constrict the sailor's arms, which would suffer from cramp in a tight fitting suit. However, it is important that the water drains from the sleeves when you fall in, or swimming becomes very difficult. Here Dee Caldwell wears shoes, and a harness with full support for his back.

Above: Three types of suits. The Long John is easier to put on with ankle zips, while the two 'shorties' are for warmer weather.

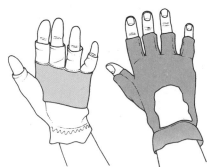

Above: You can wear mittens or gloves, but the palm should be reinforced for the wishbone.

Right: A simple windsurfing shoe and an expensive boot. It is the rubber compound that grips the board – not the tread.

Dry suits are expensive, but you should be sure to buy a good quality brand – it will give years of service.

warmer, but more expensive kind of wetsuit, is called the 'steamer'. This has special stitching which lets very little water in or out, and consequently is much warmer.

All wetsuits are made of neoprene which is double lined or single lined with brightly coloured nylon or Lycra. The double lined suits are hard wearing on both sides; the single lined suits (black on the outside) are warmer but more prone to damage.

Good wetsuits are expensive, but are a good investment which should last at least three hard seasons. Owing to the stretchiness of neoprene, fit is not usually a problem. If you're an odd size or shape, there are manufacturers who make wetsuits made-to-measure.

Boots

Some boards have a good bare foot non-slip surface, but most do not. For the learner it may be preferable to wear shoes regardless, to avoid bruising inexperienced feet.

You must find the right rubber sole compound to suit the surface of the board. Tennis shoes are fine on some, and useless on others. Alternatively you can get properly designed windsurfing shoes and boots.

Gloves

Not really necessary in the summer, when you should put up with hardening your hands.

In cold winter, neoprene mittens seem the most effective answer. They should be shaped like a fist clenched over the wishbone, with a

Wetsuits vary from the practical to the ultra chic, but it's simple black neoprene rubber that keeps you warm!

heavily reinforced palm.

Headgear

The crotch and the cranium are the two greatest areas of heat loss on the human body. In cold weather protect the head with a neoprene skull cap.

Dry suit

The dry suit is designed to keep the water out. You can get into it wearing your clothes, or more sensibly in a suit of thermal underwear, fall in the water and stay completely dry.

It has a heavy duty waterproof zip, and tight rubber seals at the neck and wrists which must be a good enough fit to be comfortable, while keeping the water out.

The dry suit is only suitable for very cold weather. It doesn't breathe, and you soon get too hot inside. It is also rather bulky and can be difficult to swim in.

Drysuits come in two styles: either proofed nylon baggy suits which have plenty of room for clothes beneath; or tighter neoprene suits which are more akin to a dry version of a wetsuit, and better suited to funboard use in strong winds and waves.

Buoyancy

Few windsurfers seem to wear buoyancy aids – they don't think the image is right!

This is nonsense. A buoyancy vest won't constrict your movements, and when you fall into the water for the umpteenth time and suddenly discover you are very tired, you will be glad of it.

Don't take any notice of the claims for buoyancy possessed by wetsuits – it's not sufficient to keep you afloat without worrying. (Wearing a dry suit is like swimming in the Dead Sea, but be careful not to invert with all the air around your feet!)

The most sensible answer may be to go for a harness with integral buoyancy (see pages 92–93) though remember the buoyancy is only equivalent to an *aid*, and is not a *lifejacket* – if you're knocked out it may float you on your face.

Carrying a Board

A board can be carried on a car roof, using a specially designed gutter rack.

This will take a couple of boards and their rigs side by side. The best way to tie them down is with webbing straps that lock on sprung teeth. The strap passes over the

The simplest roof racks attach to the gutter of the car, and can be put on and taken off very easily. Special designs are available for gutterless cars, and you can even put racks on most convertibles.

You should use special board straps at all times. Rope is not

nearly as effective, and may damage the board; while shock cords tend to be rather dangerous. The bars of the rack should have some form of padding before you put on the board (try rubber insulation tubes), with the boom and mast on top.

To tie on the board, loop the straps as shown, and tighten them through the buckles. Make sure the buckles are not in a position to rub and damage the board, and tie off the loose ends for extra security.

Properly attached you can have complete faith in a roof rack system, although it is wise to moderate your speed when driving in strong winds. Remember to tie a warning flag to each end of the mast if it overhangs.

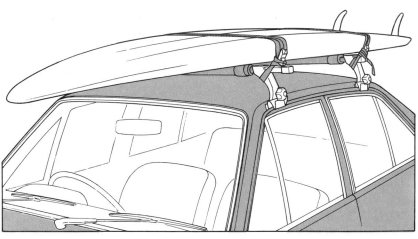

There are various ways of carrying a board down to the beach, the worst of which is carrying it under your arm. Patent trolley systems are designed to take the board, rig, and your gear but you should ensure that the wheels are big enough to cope with soft sand. It is best if you can lash your gear securely to the trolley or it will tend to come adrift, particularly with the simplest types of trolley (shown on the right).

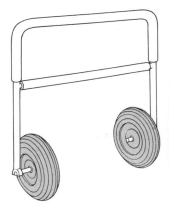

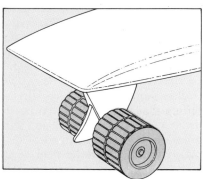

Top: A clever idea from the Hi Fly range. Little wheels slot in to the skeg boxes.

Carry the board with one hand on the dagger and the other on the mast foot which can be used as a handle (below). Hopefully production boards will get lighter and lighter in years to come — fairly soon we should expect them to weigh little more than 10 kg. A shoulder strap (above) with slings that pass under the board makes life a little easier, and was copied from the surfers. On a windy day you have to take care that you don't get whirled around like a weathercock. Carrying the board over your head (right) may solve the problem, but soon gets tiring.

board, under the rack, back again, under the rack, and locks through itself. You should take an extra turn around the mast which is placed along the centreline of the board, together with the wishbone.

You can carry as many as four or five boards, but with such a load you should accelerate, brake, and corner very gingerly.

With a very short car it may be wise to tie down either end of the board(s) to the bumpers. You can use the towing eye and skeg.

You can buy racks with built-in locking systems, which are valuable if you feel there is a chance of the board being stolen. A cheaper alternative is a continuous loop of wire which passes through a lock. This is fed through the daggerboard case and then the two ends are locked together from both sides *inside the car*. The wire is sufficiently thin to enable you to close the car doors.

To the Water

Boards are surprisingly heavy. 18 kg doesn't sound much, but it's plenty to carry over half a mile – and then you have to go back and get the rig, daggerboard etc.

The best way to carry a board is under your arm with one hand in the underside of the daggerboard case, and the other in the mast foot. If the board has a balance point mid-way this is quite easy, although you will find a short walk is far enough with a board that weighs any more than 20 kg, which is an average weight for most learner boards.

There are plenty of patent trolley systems, working around the principle of a pair of wheels on which you can push the board and rig. The trouble is that most of them get bogged down when they encounter sand – if you're going to the beach, the bigger the wheels the better. For preference, they should be shaped like footballs to keep the maximum area in contact with the sand.

Basic Theory

The theory behind windsurfing may seem a little complicated, but it you want to succeed it is worth taking the trouble to understand it.

A sail generates drive. Some of it is forward, but a lot is sideways – this is converted into forward drive for the board by means of the daggerboard.

The drive is termed the *Centre of Effort* – a point on the sail which takes the main thrust of the wind's power. The daggerboard, which resists the sideways drive, is the *Centre of Lateral Resistance*.

If the Centre of Effort (CE) balances with the Centre of Lateral Resistance (CLR), the board will be in equilibrium. In this state it is designed so that it will sail in a straight line, though no designer can allow for sea conditions.

Sail Drive

When it blows on to a correctly trimmed sail, the air flow separates and passes on either side. On the leeward side (the one furthest from the wind) the air flow is accelerated by the curve which has been built into the sail. The result is a reduction in air pressure. The high pressure area on the windward side of the sail (closest to the wind) then pushes toward the low pressure, and thus generates drive.

The drive is roughly at right angles to the chord of the sail – an imaginary line drawn between the clew (where the end of the sail meets the wishbone) and the mast. Its efficiency in propelling the board will obviously depend on your course in relation to the wind:

Close hauled
Sailing towards the wind, you would expect to be pushed sideways and backwards. The aerodynamic shape of the daggerboard combats this tendency, converting movement into forward drive.

There are exceptions to this general rule. Experts can sail strong wind boards on a close hauled course with a single skeg to combat leeway (moving sideways). However speed is imperative. The board must be planing in a minimum wind strength of Force 4, and even then the sailor's technique will be critical.

Reaching
When the wind is on the beam there is less sideways drive and less pressure on the daggerboard. Consequently, this is always the fastest point of sailing.

Running
One would expect sailing with the wind behind to give the most drive. Not so – the wind is only hitting the sail on one side, and consequently there is no area of low pressure. The sail is simply pushed along rather than sucked, while the air flow round the edges suffers from turbulence.

Apparent Wind

The *apparent wind* is the wind *experienced by the sailor*, and is not the same as *true wind*, which is the wind *experienced by someone standing still*.

If a windsurfer is sailing towards a true wind of 15 knots at a board speed of five knots, he will be experiencing an apparent wind speed of nearly 20 knots. However, if he were sailing away from a true wind of 15 knots, we would need to deduct his board speed (say 5 knots) to find the strength of the apparent wind on his sail (10 knots). This is less than the true wind, and combined with no aerodynamic suck on his sail, running becomes a slow point of sailing.

The faster a board sails, the more the apparent wind will change in direction, blowing increasingly from ahead. Thus a board travelling at high speed will need to trim its sail far tighter than one travelling slowly, even though the true wind remains constant in its direction and power.

Sail Trim

The sail's drive is determined by its camber, which is the degree of fullness in the sail and its trim. To find the correct angle of attack, the sail should be trimmed so that its chord is no closer than 15–20 degrees to the apparent wind. If it is closer, the air flow will break away into turbulence to leeward, which will brake rather than suck the sail. On the other hand, if it is not sheeted in enough, all the air flow will shift to the leeward side, and the whole sail will lift and lose efficiency.

Eventually you will be able to trim the sail by instinct. You will find you also need to tune the amount of camber, which can be adjusted by tightening the outhaul and downhaul. With a bendy mast and the shape already cut into the sail, the pull on the leech and luff can be used to change a sail from full to flat to suit the conditions.

For a learner a full sail should be used for light breezes, and it should be trimmed flat as the wind increases for easy handling.

Board Shape

Apart from sail drive, a board's performance is also affected by several other factors. To perform to maximum advantage it must be in perfect balance. This will be determined by: the size and position of the skeg(s); the size, shape, and position of the daggerboard; the distance between the daggerboard and the skeg(s); the distance between the mast step and the stern; the design of the rig; and the design of the board.

Board shape and design is limited, and will normally be a mixture of a square, pin, or round-tail outline, allied with a bottom that is flat, triangular, concave, or round.

Many factors contribute to steering the board. In addition to steering with the rig, a strong wind funboard can be 'footsteered' using the shape of the tail.

Steering the Board

We have seen that a windsurfer is balanced by the correct design of the board and rig. The sailor keeps control by varying the relationship between the CE and CLR.

By tilting the rig forward, the CE is moved forward of the CLR. This pushes the board's nose away from the wind (ie it bears off). Conversely, by tilting the rig aft, the board's stern is pushed away from the wind (it heads up).

This basic theory behind steering a course is tempered by many factors: your board will never be in 100 percent perfect balance; the sea will affect the board's course; and a puff of wind will shift the CE further aft. You will learn that if you luff the rig (let the sail out) the board will head up, and if you sheet in it will bear away – the CE moves aft and forward respectively.

When you are running straight downwind, steering with the rig is somewhat different. The CE points directly forward, while the CLR points aft, so you tilt the rig to one side or the other rather than backwards or forwards. If you tilt it to the windward side the board will bear away; and if you tilt it to leeward it will head up.

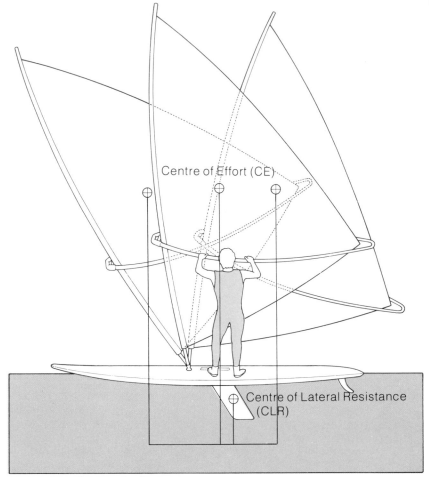

Centre of Effort (CE)

Centre of Lateral Resistance (CLR)

Above: The Centre of Effort is the fulcrum of the wind's force on the sail. If it is directly over the Centre of Lateral Resistance, the board will travel in a straight line. Rake the CE forward of the CLR, and it will push the nose away from the wind. Rake it aft, and it will push the stern away from the wind so that you head up.

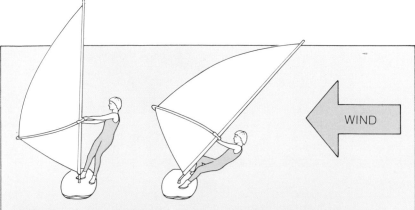

WIND

When the wind increases, the sailor is unable to hold the rig in the upright position. This is the point where a conventional sailcraft would begin to heel away from the wind. The boardsailor heels the rig into the wind, and hangs beneath it, with his weight supported by the pull of the sail, while his board remains flat.

The sailor hangs on to the rig with his Centre of Gravity well outboard. The push of the mast foot will make the board heel away from him, but his feet will act as a counterbalance.

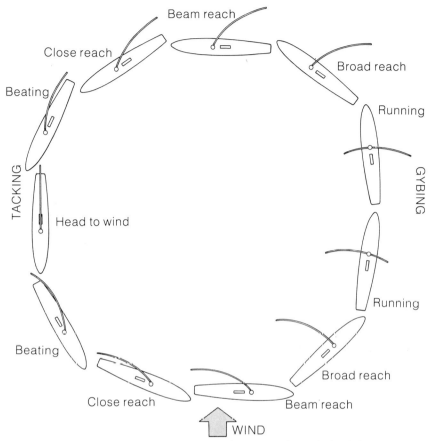

Above: The points of sailing, travelling in a complete circle. It is very necessary practice for a learner to be able to sail in any direction – not just downwind, which is easiest when you begin, and the most difficult point when you get better and take on strong winds.

Balancing the Wind

A yacht heels over as the force of the wind increases, effectively cutting down its sail area and drive. As well as losing drive, it also loses keel area (CLR) and makes greater leeway (moving sideways rather than forwards).

In the case of the windsurfer, however, it is the rig rather than the hull that is inclined, but in the direction the wind is coming from. The same drive continues, but with less projected sail area; the efficiency of the CLR continues; and at the same time the rig generates 'lift' to make the board lighter and faster.

The more it blows, the more you cant the rig to windward, with your weight hanging beneath it. It takes a lot of faith to lean back and let the rig carry you, but in anything over Force 3 it becomes essential to windsurfing.

Conclusions

Once you have mastered the principle of CE and CLR, you will realise that the remainder of board control is a compromise – between the board's design, the rig, the conditions, and your technique. Only experience can give you all the answers.

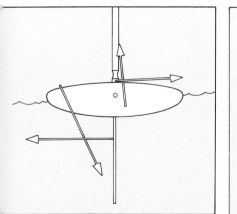

As well as the mast foot, the motion of the long daggerboard through the water will also make the board heel away from the wind, particularly when it is blowing hard. A retracting dagger will help.

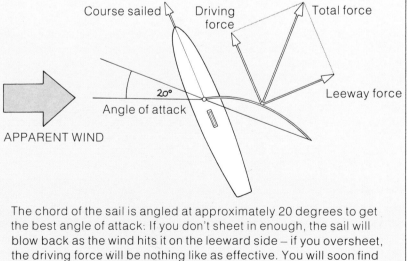

The chord of the sail is angled at approximately 20 degrees to get the best angle of attack: If you don't sheet in enough, the sail will blow back as the wind hits it on the leeward side – if you oversheet, the driving force will be nothing like as effective. You will soon find the correct sheeting angle instinctively.

First Attempts

You've got the board, you understand the basics, and now you're ready to try windsurfing.

First, choose your day! The most important factors will be weather and the place you intend to sail from. If they are unsuitable, you stand a fair chance of wasting your time. Don't go out if it's freezing cold; blowing too hard or flat calm with no wind; or if there are waves breaking on the beach. Any of these factors will be enough to put you off if it's your first attempt.

Offshore Winds

The great danger for a learner on a windsurfer is being blown away from the shore. An offshore wind blowing off the land will get progressively stronger as you get further out. If you find you can't cope, you will spend more and more time falling into the water with the wind pushing you in a direction you don't want to go, at an ever-increasing speed. The end result is that you will eventually need to be rescued.

Therefore, if you're sailing on open water, always beware of an offshore wind. Near to the shore it will be broken up by obstacles, such as trees and houses, making gusty, difficult conditions; further out it may be a lot stronger than you bargained for.

However, an onshore wind may be just as unsatisfactory. The wind heaps up waves, and depending on how the shore shelves, this can easily build up into surf with a fierce undertow – conditions which can be handled by experienced sailors alone – otherwise the all too frequent results are broken masts, wishbones and daggerboards.

Even small waves will present a problem, because on your first attempts you will find the board quite unstable enough on flat calm water – and you don't want to make this any worse.

The ideal compromise is when the wind is blowing more or less parallel to the shore, and coming from a direction that is unobstructed. The wind won't be gusty and the water will be flat, and if its direction is slightly angled onshore it will blow you home in the end. If it's not, you should check that there is a lee shore (one that the wind is blowing on to) at an angle to the shore you are sailing off.

Tides

Tides are just as dangerous as offshore winds. Unless you research an area thoroughly before you sail in it, there is no way of telling if there is any tide, and where and how fast it runs. Tides frequently run at as much as four knots, and can create conditions that only a very experienced sailor can get out of.

The answer is to establish in advance whether the tide is going out or coming in (High Water is normally followed by Low Water with an interval of about six hours. It then takes another six hours to build up to High Water once again.) You should also find out if certain states of the tide are unsafe.

(You will do well to establish whether there is a two mile walk over the beach to the sea at Low Water. When you're carrying a board this will seem a long way – you'll wish you'd worked this sort of thing out before you decided to go off sailing.)

Cold

Cold is the beginner's great enemy, particularly in Northern countries.

The effect of cold water and a chilling wind can have an alarming effect on your body heat, lowering it critically before you realize what has happened. This condition, called hypothermia, is dangerous for beginners who spend a lot of time falling in the water, and then sitting on their boards getting colder and colder. As the hypothermia worsens, the victim becomes increasingly unable to cope: strength fails; reflexes slow; and willpower decreases.

For this reason it is imperative to dress correctly and sensibly. Wear a wetsuit, boots, and a windproof top on any day when there is the remotest chance of getting cold – it's better to overheat and be sensible.

Inshore Water

Inshore waters might seem most suitable to the beginner. There is always a lee shore not too far away, and so long as the piece of water is relatively small, it hardly matters if the wind is offshore from where you start off.

However, some stretches of inland water are quite large, and it doesn't take many things to go wrong before you can find yourself in serious trouble.

Unless the country is very low-lying, the wind is liable to be gusty, owing to obstructions on shore. In addition, the water may be considerably colder, and far less buoyant than seawater. A fitful wind and very cold water is a prime cause of hypothermia. (In fact the first windsurfing fatality in the UK occurred in just these conditions in the Lake District – and the victim was not wearing a wetsuit.)

Weather Forecasts

How do you judge if the weather will be suitable? First, you should look out for weather forecasts that are designed for yachtsmen. There are numerous shipping forecasts on the radio throughout the day, and these should always be posted up by sailing clubs. Or you can look in a newspaper or telephone a weather centre.

It really helps if your first attempts can be made on a nice sunny day with a light breeze. At first, rigging will seem complicated, but you soon find that once you can rig one board, you can rig them all in little more than five minutes.

Seamanship

Before you take to the water, you must understand the basics of seamanship, and particularly the *Rules of the Road*. Showing courtesy to others while afloat is a major safety factor.

'Rules of the Road'

The rules of the road are designed to stop boats hitting one another. They apply to tankers, yachts, speed boats, dinghies, and windsurfers – in fact anything on the water.

The rules of the road for windsurfers are internationally recognized – they're the same as the ones for yachts. They are simple to understand and not at all like the more complex rules used for racing.

1. A board on starboard tack has right of way over one on port tack.

You are on starboard tack when the wind is coming from the starboard side. If you find this difficult to remember, some wishbone coverings are green on one side (starboard) and red on the other (port – remember the colour of the drink).

2. The overtaking craft must keep clear.

(This is a matter of courtesy. However life becomes increasingly less courteous once you become involved in racing.)

3. When two craft on the same tack are converging, the one to leeward has right of way.

In effect this means that the craft sailing a higher course has right of way – if you are reaching, and the other chap is beating to windward with both of you on the same tack, you give way.

Meeting Other Craft

The above three basic rules will serve when you meet another windsurfer. In principle they should apply when you meet any type of sailing yacht.

The written exception is when the other yacht is having to negotiate a channel, and would be put aground or on the rocks if you tried to enforce your right of way. However, there are other important *unwritten* exceptions which depend on your commonsense and courtesy.

1. Craft that are racing have right of way over ones that are not.

This is because every inch counts when you're racing, and if a racer has to change course he may lose ground and places to his rivals, while for someone who's out on a jaunt it really doesn't matter.

Therefore, if it's easy for you to give way (even though he's on port and you're on starboard) you would be sensible to do so gracefully; if not, you are under no obligation to do so. (Remember that people who race sometimes get extremely aggressive and overheated, and assume they have right of way over *anything* on the water. This is most certainly not the case, and you don't automatically have to get out of the way just because someone yells 'I'm racing'.)

The rules for racing sailboats are a study in themselves. There are very many of them and they are very complex – you need a book specifically on the subject.

2. Larger craft have the right of way over smaller ones.

It is a written rule that pleasure craft give right of way to commercial craft – never try to mix it with an oil tanker!

However, your windsurfer does have the right of way over a hundred-foot schooner if you are on starboard and he is on port.

It would be patently ridiculous to insist on this. You can change course in seconds, while for the yacht it will be a major undertaking. Therefore on principle it is a sensible idea to reckon on generally giving way to all cabin craft, keel boats etc (though not if they are stupid and inconsiderate enough to barge through a windsurfer race

course). Remember that you are probably sailing the most nimble, easily manoeuvred craft on the water, and give way accordingly.

3. Others may not understand the Rules of the Road.

It pays to assume that others are not so well informed as you are, or simply don't know what course you are steering – a novice windsurfer often sails in an unpredictably variable direction. If a speedboat is heading straight at you he should certainly give way, but it would be foolish to take it for granted that he will.

Similarly, if you are steering unpredictably you can hardly expect another craft to know which way to turn in order not to foul you.

4. Don't make a nuisance of yourself on beaches or with swimmers.

Remember that dragging a rig over people's heads doesn't go down well, and a board can be extremely dangerous. Left on the beach upside down, someone is liable to trip over it, and on the water the bow or the skeg could be lethal for a swimmer, if you're careering around partly out of control.

Because of this you will find local bylaws that prohibit windsurfing in certain places, both inland and on the coast. Busy beaches have areas set aside, with windsurfing lanes to get boards away from the swimmers.

Commonsense

Both sea and inland waters can be very unfriendly to a lonely little figure on a windsurfer. So, when you first try windsurfing:

1. Check the weather.
2. Check the area.
3. Check the safety facilities.
4. Ensure someone knows what you are doing.
5. Wear the right clothing.
6. Know the rules of the road.
7. Don't bite off more than you can chew, for unintentional rescue is ignominy.

The Beaufort Scale

The wind is measured on the Beaufort Scale, invented by Admiral Beaufort in 1805. The units are knots, which are nautical miles (about 1.85 kilometres) per hour. These descriptions are for life on the open sea. It won't be quite so extreme close inshore, which is windsurfer territory, but it would be highly unusual for most people to sail effectively in Force 7 or 8.

Force 0
1 knot or less. Calm. Mirror-like sea.

Force 1
1–3 knots. Light air. Gently scaly ripples.

Force 2
4–6 knots. Light breeze. Small wavelets. May have glassy crests but these will not break.

Force 3
7–10 knots. Gentle breeze: large wavelets. Crests begin to break. Possibly some white horses.

Force 4
11–16 knots. Moderate breeze. Waves becoming longer with white horses.

Force 5
17–21 knots. Fresh breeze. Moderate waves with white horses and possibly occasional spray.

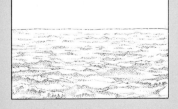

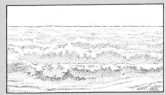

Force 6
22–27 knots. Strong breeze. Large waves forming with extensive white crests and spray.

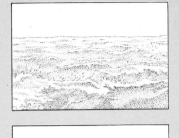

Force 7
28–33 knots. Near gale. Sea heaps up and foam from breaking waves blows in streaks.

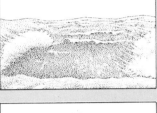

Force 8
34–40 knots. Gale. Moderately high waves. Edge of crests break into spindrift. Well marked streaks.

Force 9
41–47 knots. Severe gale. High waves. Confused breaking crests. Spray affects visibility.

Force 10
48–55 knots. Storm. Very high waves with long overhanging crests. Sea surface becomes white.

Force 11
56–63 knots. Violent storm. Exceptionally high waves hiding ships from view. Sea covered in white foam.

Force 12
64 knots plus. Hurricane. Air full of driving spray. Very bad visibility.

Understanding the Weather

A windsurfer is interested in wind – as you become more proficient you'll curse the weather if there isn't enough of it!

However, you may also run into problems if there is too much wind, and for this reason it is important to have some basic understanding of the weather – at least enough to be able to interpret weather forecasts.

Getting Information

Many weather forecasts – on the TV, radio, and in the newspapers – are designed for people on land, and provide limited information for sailing. You will learn a lot more from shipping and inshore water forecasts which will give you the visibility, wind strength in knots, and the likely weather pattern.

Even better, telephone a local Weather Centre. The major ones are manned 24 hours a day, and the forecaster will normally be quite happy to chat to you about your windsurfing prospects.

Wind

Wind is created by differences in atmospheric pressure; and the effect of the land and sea being heated up by the sun.

Highs and lows

When atmospheric pressure is high (called a *high* or anticyclone) the weather is settled and the wind tends to be light. When it is low (called a *low* or depression) you can expect strong winds.

Highs tend to stay pretty much where they are, while lows usually move along fast, with the worst weather (for those on land) right under their centre.

However, the amount of wind depends on the pressure difference (pressure is measured in *millibars*, which is why all yachtsmen watch the barometer) between the *high* and the *low*, as the wind always tends to blow from the former to the latter, and not the other way round.

Sun and sea

The direction and strength of the wind is governed by the atmospheric difference between the *high* and *low*, as the *low* draws wind from the *high*. However this effect is tempered by local conditions, and in particular the effect of the sun as it heats up the land and sea each day.

Every morning the sun heats up the air over the land more quickly than the air over the sea. The hot air from the land starts to rise, and this creates a low pressure area which draws the much cooler air from the sea towards it – in this way an early morning onshore breeze is created. Obviously, this steadily increasing onshore wind is perfect for windsurfing.

As the sun begins to go down, the wind starts to drop, and in a stable weather pattern it will continue to get lighter and lighter. As the sun disappears the land will then cool very rapidly, and reverse the pattern of the morning. A new low pressure area over the water (now warmer than the land) draws the cool air from the land, and an offshore wind builds up.

Exceptions and Dangers

Most areas will have their local weather idiosyncracies. Sometimes these will be quite marked, and you should always do a little preliminary weather research before you sail on an unknown stretch of water.

When there are mountainous areas inland, you can expect the wind to funnel down valleys and blow extremely hard at very short notice. The *Mistral*, which blows down the Rhone Valley to the French Mediterranean, is typical of this – one minute, a steady breeze; five minutes later, a full Force 6.

The Mistral comes suddenly and often unexpectedly, blowing down the Rhône Valley into the Mediterranean. It is an offshore wind which frequently catches out sailors on the south coast of France, and can therefore be very dangerous. Telltale signs are a very clear blue sky with long thin cigar shaped clouds low on the horizon. This sailor has a long journey home in a Force 7 wind.

You should also beware when there are mountains or steep hills on the shoreline. With acute differences in temperature on the slopes caused by sunny and shady areas, you may experience sudden and violent downdraughts.

Inland Waters
The sea breeze/land breeze syndrome is primarily of interest to those who sail on the open sea.

Apart from the central European and American lakes, few stretches of inland water are large enough for it to have much effect. Their weather pattern is more likely to be changed by the surrounding houses and countryside.

Getting Caught
High temperature and a humid atmosphere cause air to shoot up to a height of around five miles, where

it cools very rapidly. The moisture then condenses into rain or hail, and is accompanied by violent gusts and static electricity lightning.

What's happened? It's a thunderstorm, and there will be plenty of warning signs before it happens. When thick cumulus clouds start to soar skywards in a dark tower you know what's coming and you know what to do – get back to the shore or it will catch you on the open sea.

Unpacking the Board

It's an exciting moment when you take delivery of your first board. However, don't get so carried away that you fail to check all the items. All boards should have similar elements.

The board itself
Probably wrapped in heavy duty polythene. This may come in handy for storing the board in the winter.

The skeg
Most skegs are fitted into a 'universal' fin box, held in with a lug at one end and bolt and plate at the other. This makes them easily interchangeable.

Occasionally you will find a board with a skeg that is screwed directly into the bottom – it's cheaper for the manufacturer, but not so good for you.

The daggerboard
On some you will have to adjust the 'shims'. These are the friction pads that control how tightly the daggerboard fits in its box. Be careful not to overdo this as it will loosen up in the water with use.

The universal joint
This is attached to the *mast foot*, which comes in a variety of shapes and sizes. The top half plugs into the base of the mast, and there should always be some facility for leashing it to the board.

The mast
Either glassfibre or alloy, which may be in two pieces that sleeve together. With some glassfibre masts there is a separate mast tip.

The wishbone
Rubber covered alloy. There are cleats for the outhaul and inhaul lines, and occasionally you are expected to screw these into position.

The sail
Most sails have three or more battens, and these are surprisingly easy to lose. Try to roll the sail or fold it

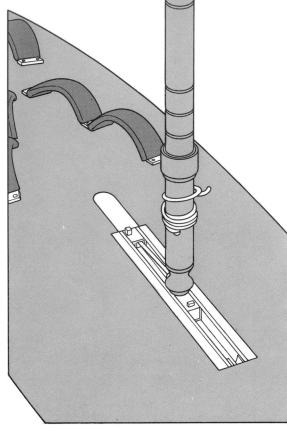

More expensive boards are fitted with sliding mast tracks and adjustable mast extensions (above). These are useful refinements which are appreciated by more experienced sailors. The mast foot and universal joint (right) is surprisingly complex when disassembled. Try to keep the nuts free from salt water corrosion.

along its original creases.

More high performance sails tend to have full length battens. Their advantages are only felt in stronger winds, and they are not important for the beginner.

Manufacturers' Variations
Some parts are interchangeable between marques – others are not. To change rigs, one simply has to mate the universal joint with the mast foot that fits a particular board. Most wishbones can be used with any rig if they are the right length (some are adjustable). Universal system fins are normally interchangeable.

Right: Getting boards ready on the beach of Hookipa in Hawaii. At the top level of the sport windsurfing is extremely hi-tech, with constant updates and refinements in accessories and equipment that filter down to beginners.

Assembling the Rig

When it comes to assembling the rig, most systems are very similar. Many new boards are sold with full rigging instructions – if they are not, it should be fairly simple to work out any variations.

● The sleeve of the sail is slid over the mast, leaving the base of the mast (the broad part) sticking out of the bottom. Most masts are a single length.

● The universal joint/mast foot is pushed into the base of the mast.

● The downhaul line is tied and lightly tensioned between the tack of the sail and the mast foot. You will need at least a 3:1 purchase, and there is sometimes a roller and cleat mounted on the mast foot for this purpose. If not, you can make a loop at the bottom of the inhaul line with a bowline.

● Next you attach the boom to the mast with the inhaul line. There are all sorts of methods of achieving a tight fit, and the one you use will be governed by the design of your boom end fitting. For a beginner the easiest way is often to use the simple inhaul lashing shown in the **Useful Knots** diagram, with the free end passed through the holes in the boom, round the mast, and secured on the cleat provided.

An alternative simple method is to tie a figure-of-eight stopper knot in the end of the line. Pull it through one of the holes in the boom end, twice round the mast, back up through the other hole, and back onto the cleat.

● While doing this, it is imperative that the boom lies parallel to the mast, with the end by the mast foot. When you straighten the boom it then has the effect of tightening the inhaul.

You can then attach and tension the outhaul – once again the

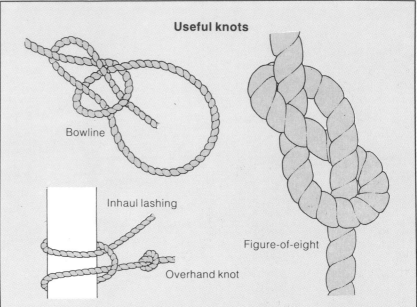

Useful knots

Bowline

Inhaul lashing

Overhand knot

Figure-of-eight

The bowline and figure-of-eight are useful knots. The inhaul lashing shown is very simple. Sometimes both free ends of the line are tied into a single overhand knot which fits in a notch in the boom end.

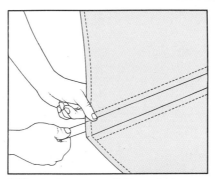

1 The battens are slid into their pockets and are then held in by a fold of the sailcloth.

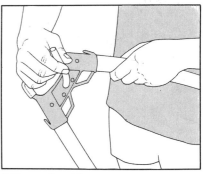

2 The uphaul line is attached to the wishbone. It is usually passed through a hole and knotted.

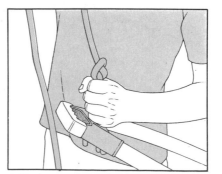

3 Tie knots down the length of the uphaul line to act as hand-holds to pull it up with.

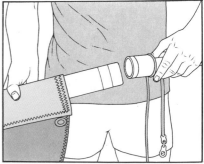

4 When sliding the universal joint into the mast, there must be no sand or it will get jammed.

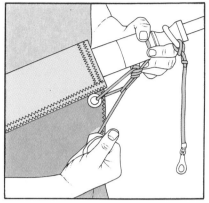

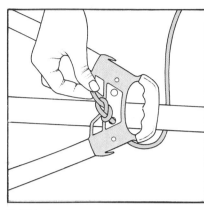

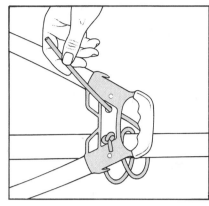

5 The downhaul attaches the clew to the universal joint. It tensions the luff of the sail and governs its shape with the outhaul.

6 This is an easy way to tie the inhaul, starting with a figure-of-eight and the boom alongside the mast.

7 Take the free end twice round the mast and back through the other hole; then pull through the cleat.

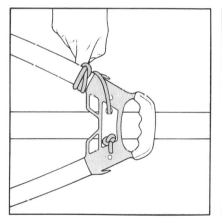

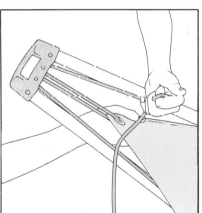

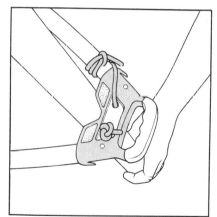

8 Pull it as tight as possible, and tie the free end off neatly so that it cannot flap around and annoy you.

9 Use the outhaul to pull down the boom until it's perpendicular to the mast. The inhaul will self-tighten.

10 Some inhaul fittings are so effective that you have to take care not to crush the mast.

method will be governed by the design of the end fitting.

● If the sail has full length battens it is easiest to slide them into their pockets after tensioning the outhaul. They usually have a webbing strap and buckle.

If the sail has short battens, it is easiest to put them in before rigging the sail. They are usually held in place by a fold in the sailcloth.

● Attach the uphaul rope. A short length of shockcord normally secures it to the mast foot.

● Tension the outhaul and downhaul lines until the sail takes up its correct aerofoil shape.

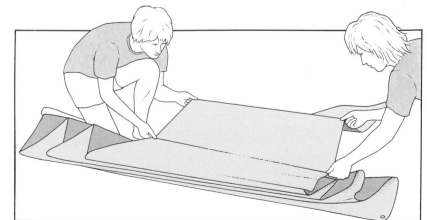

Above: 'Flaking' the sail. Take parallel folds while holding the sail on the leech and luff, folding first one way and then the other. Always keep the folds in the same place if possible.

Practice Ashore

Before you take to the water, you can set up the board and the rig on dry land. You can then ensure that everything is correctly set up, and try out the various exercises that you are going to have to do on the water.

You can either place the board flat on the ground with the skeg removed, and then attach the rig to it; or simply stick the mast foot into the ground, without bothering with the board.

You can then try pulling up the rig; walking around it; and sheeting it in and out. By doing this you will get the feel of it before you start, making sure that the wishbone is at the correct height, and that you like the look of the sail.

Setting Up the Rig

It is important that the sail has been set correctly. In moderate conditions of around Force 2 this should require reasonable tension on the downhaul, with the outhaul pulled out within a couple of inches of the end of the wishbone. If there are bad creases, something is very wrong – either with the way you have set the sail (you have most probably overtightened it) or possibly with the sail itself (rather un-likely).

If there are vertical creases, either try tensioning the outhaul, or let off a little downhaul. If there are horizontal creases, try tensioning the downhaul, or let off a little outhaul. If there are creases along the batten pockets, tension the battens.

Sails can be set full or flat, though the amount of fullness is determined primarily by the sail's cut. For a beginner the sail should be set flatter as the wind gets stronger, but the most important consideration is that it maintains a stable shape with the centre of

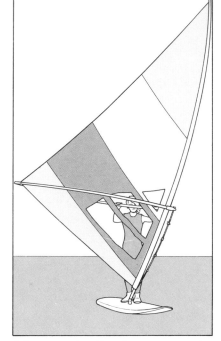

1 By removing the skeg you can rig the board and practice on dry land before you take to the water.

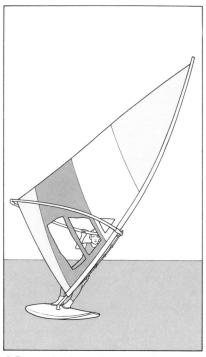

2 Place the board across the wind, lean back a little and then sheet in to get the feel of the wind.

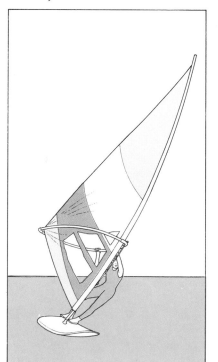

3 Sheet in a little more and you are 'sailing', leaning back further as the wind increases.

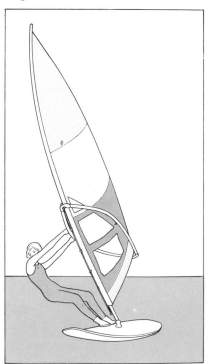

4 Turn the board and try the other tack. (Alternatively you could just bury the mast foot in the sand).

effort staying in one position.

It's unfortunate that many cheaper rigs tend to be unstable when compared to expensive hi-tech equipment that feature stiff masts and full length battens. However this situation is improving with increasingly refined manufac-turing techniques, as developments at the top end of the sport percolate through to the mass market.

So long as the sail sets well and is easy to use, the beginner shouldn't worry too much about rig refine-ments – they are really only impor-tant in strong winds.

You should carry the rig over your head, with the wishbone pointing directly into the direction the wind is coming from. Keep it level, and don't let the wind get under or on top of it.

Balancing
You must get the hang of balancing on the board before you try sailing it, with and without the daggerboard. Unless you're a surfer, it will seem difficult at first, though you'll soon get used to it. Try doing it in small waves as well – it's all good practice.

Balancing
Carry the board down to the water. The easiest way is with one hand in the daggerboard case, and the other in the mast foot well.

You can then try standing on it and balancing, with and without the daggerboard. Also try paddling it – when you are inexperienced, it may be the only way to get home.

Carrying the Rig
When you intend to go sailing, leave the board by the water's edge and put the rig in the water first. Left unattended the board would be blown away quite rapidly, whereas the rig is part submerged and drifts very slowly.

The best way to carry the rig is over your head with the luff of the sail facing the direction the wind is coming from. You must always keep it flat and facing in this direc-tion, or the wind is liable to take control and turn you into an in-voluntary hang-glider.

Fixing the Mast Foot
Take the board into the water alongside the rig, and attach the mast foot. It must be a very tight fit which will only come out if there is a lot of pressure – for example if the mast or one of your limbs will break if it doesn't.

Having a mast foot that comes out at inopportune moments is in-credibly frustrating, and can be dangerous. Most modern mast feet can be tightened or loosened, or alternatively you can wrap the mast foot with insulating tape to pad it out and make it a perfect fit – this was always necessary on the old Windsurfer wooden T-pieces.

Leashing the Mast Foot
The mast foot must be leashed to the hull, so that if it comes out, it is still attached to the board. Most modern boards have a leashing system with a shock cord, but if it's not provided you must improvise with a short length of line.

Getting Under Way

When you get started, the board should be in deep enough water for you to put in the whole length of the daggerboard – standing by the board, the water need not come up any higher than your thighs.

Before you hop on the board it's best to line it up so that everything is set for getting under way; you want the wind blowing on to your back with the rig lying away from you.

At first, just hold the uphaul line with one hand, and try and get comfortably balanced before you attempt to pull up the rig.

Find out the most comfortable position for your feet as well as your body. On most boards they should be close together on the centreline of the board, just between the mast foot and the daggerboard case. On some boards you can put a foot forward of the mast, which will help to keep the rig inclined forwards; others won't have enough buoyancy in the bow, and you will have to keep your weight back to avoid submarining when under way.

When you pull up the rig, you will be amazed by how heavy it seems. The sail and the mast sleeve are full of water, and with the wind holding the sail down it seems like a ton weight until it's clear of the water. Getting over this is simply a matter of technique, but for a beginner it always makes it important to have an undersized sail.

Once you've got the clew clear of the water, rest and get comfortably balanced once again. You can then stop and work out where the wind is coming from. Then incline the rig fore and aft, which will turn the board in the direction you require.

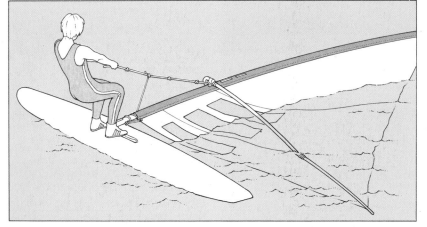

Pulling up the rig. Place your feet close together on the centreline of the board. It's normally easiest if one is just aft of the mast while the other is in front of it. Then take the uphaul line.

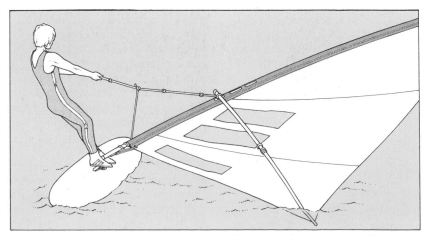

Make sure the wind is behind you and pull the rig a little way out of the water. If it is not on the beam, the board and rig will now slew around until it is. Lean back against the weight of the rig.

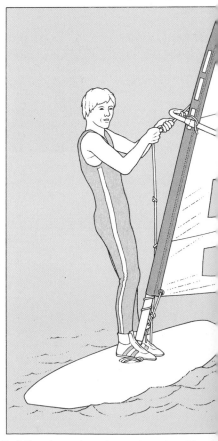

Pull the rig up hand over hand until the clew is clear of the water. It will seem very heavy. The sleeve is full of water which drains away once it is upright, and while the clew drags, the wind will hold it down against the water. Therefore it's less tiring to pull it up quickly.

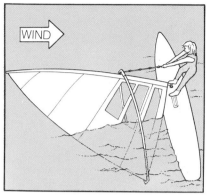

1 If the wind is downwind (to leeward) uphauling is relatively simple. However it may be to windward (pointing towards the wind as shown).

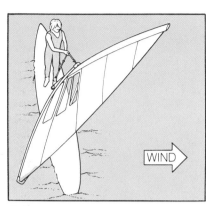

2 If you pull the mast tip a little way clear, the wind will begin to slew round both rig and board. Once the clew is clear, it will swing across the tail of the board.

Getting going: By this time you will have fallen, and the board will inevitably blow downwind of the rig. You must learn how to uphaul with the rig on the wrong side, and eventually you will discover how you can walk the board round in a full circle.

The correct position for getting underway is with the rig at 90 degrees to the board. Leaning the rig forward makes the board bear away; leaning it back makes the board head up. Let go of the uphaul and hold the rig with one hand on the mast. When you feel comfortable bring the rig across your body and swivel to face forward in one movement. Note the way the rig is leaning into the wind in the last three drawings. This is necessary to prevent luffing.

Place the back hand on the boom followed by the front hand, but keep the rig leaning over all the time. Then pull back evenly with both arms to power the sail.

If the board starts to luff up towards the wind lean the rig further over (to the left hand 'windward' side), and try pulling in more on the back hand.

When you want to stop, let go with the back hand which will depower the rig and return to position **4**. If you want to stop in a hurry, you can simply drop the rig.

3 The rig will always behave like a flag if you hold it with a loose grip. By leaning it to one side or the other you can turn the board through a complete circle.

4 The rig is in the right position when it's at right angles blowing downwind from the board. Hold it with your front hand on the mast and get your balance.

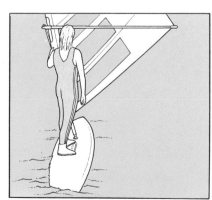

5 Pull the rig well over to windward, at the same time swivelling to face forward. Note the comfortable and relaxed stance.

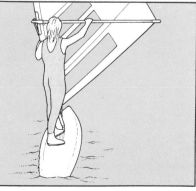

6 Reach out and grasp the boom with your back hand. Continue to keep the rig inclined to windward and at right angles to the board.

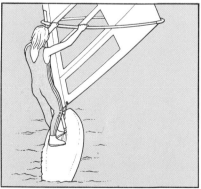

7 Place your front hand on the boom, and pull in evenly with both arms which will power the sail and get you moving. Lean back.

Sailing a Course

When you try getting under way, the wind must be on the beam, blowing across the board at right angles. There is no need to hurry, for the procedure can be followed step-by-step, with pauses in between the stages. All the time you must rest and get the feel of what you're doing until you feel comfortable: holding the rig with the uphaul line; holding the rig with your mast hand; and holding the wishbone with both hands.

Once you start sailing a course, you will find out the best way of holding the wishbone. In moderate winds you will want the mast hand to be around six inches behind the mast, with the boom hand another 18 inches or so further back. The CE will be centred right in the middle, between your hands, and if you feel uncomfortable and unbalanced you must move your hands

Remember that once you are sailing, you have to observe the Rules of the Road, whether or not you are in control of the board.

In this instance, starboard (the dinghy) has right of way over port (the windsurfer). This should be tempered with common sense.

Bearing away

To bear away, the sailor needs to rake the rig forward, while gradually sheeting out the sail and inclining it to windward as the wind goes further behind. When the wind is directly behind (running) you sail with the rig at right angles to it (**4**).

You need to keep your balance.

Foot position is important, and you must move your weight inboard as the sideways pull on the sail slackens. It helps to give some sharp pulls with the sheet hand to help the board bear away. You will also find that you can help a conventional board bear away if you push down the windward side.

1

2

3

1   2   3   4

Heading up

To head up, you rake the rig aft, sheeting in until you are on a beat. In light winds you will then have the wishbone close to your body with your arms bent.

The beat is a difficult point of sailing for the learner. You must sail as close as possible to the

wind, without going so close that the wind begins to strike the sail on the leeward side and the board rounds up so that it is facing directly into the wind (**4**).

In light winds, sail with the rig raked a little forward; your arms bent; and the sail just starting to flutter a very little.

4

until you find the correct position. As it blows harder you will need to shift your grip as the CE moves further aft, and you can experiment by grasping the boom with an over and underhand grip – whichever feels better.

Altering Course

You can alter course on a board as easily and rapidly as with the rudder on a boat. Weather conditions make a difference. If it's blowing hard with big waves and you're sailing a sensitive board with a rounded hull, it will react instantaneously.

Altering course works basically on the principle of CE over CLR. If you want to head up into the wind you rake the rig aft; if you want to bear away from the wind you rake it forward. Once you are on the desired new course, get the rig back into its original position, which will

be inclined slightly forward, and trim the sail accordingly. Next, practise sailing a wavy course – heading up and bearing away.

The Points of Sailing

1. Running. Travelling in the same direction as the wind.

There is no suction on the sail and the effect of the wind is ameliorated. To steer, you must bank the sail to either side.

2. Reaching. The wind on or nearly on the beam, and less pressure on the daggerboard makes this the fastest and easiest point of sailing. If the wind is coming from behind it is a broad reach; if it is coming from ahead it is a close reach.

3. Beating. Sailing as close to the wind as possible in order to claw up to windward. Depending on your skill and your board, you can normally sail within 30 degrees of the direction the wind is coming from.

Tacking

In order to sail towards the direction the wind is coming from, you need to sail a zig-zag course. This is called tacking.

As you try to reach the point you wish to get to, you sail on one tack and then on the other (port and starboard) as it suits you. Governing factors on the tacks you choose are liable to be the prevailing conditions, obstructions en route, or simply tacking for the sake of a change.

Your port and starboard tacks should be contained within a maximum arc of around 90 degrees – any more, and you will sail a very long way to get to where you want.

As you get more experienced, the arc between your tacks should come down to around 60 degrees, depending on how close to the wind the board you sail will point. This is governed by the board itself – the efficiency of its rig, its shape, and its daggerboard, allied to weather conditions – as well as your skill. You must sail the board close to the wind, but not too close or it will lose power and stall as the wind comes increasingly on the leeward side of the sail.

Judging just how close to sail is largely a matter of experience and technique, but a board will always head up into the wind when inexperienced hands are not keeping the rig raked far enough forwards. The telltale sign is when the sail begins to 'lift' – the wind on the leeward side will start pushing the area around the window in the sail towards you. Unless you react and bear away, the board will continue to round up and eventually deposit you in the water.

When you change tacks, your

There are many ways of tacking, and as you get more experienced your technique will get more refined and change a little to suit every occasion.

For a fairly fast tack you head up by raking the rig aft (**1**). Continue raking it aft until the clew is over the centreline of the board (**2**) which will soon be facing directly into the wind (**3**). At this point transfer your front hand to the mast, a few inches from the wishbone. Then start to move round the front of the mast, transferring your other hand to the mast as you do so, and continuing to rake the rig aft (**4**). Move round the other side of the board, while the clew swings over the stern and into the wind (**5**).

WIND

movements should be smooth and unfussy. The object is to get the board sailing on the opposite tack, and you don't need to stick rigidly to a set of rules in order to do so.

All you want to do is to turn the board through the eye of the wind, and then start off again on your new tack. At first you can simply swing the rig round the stern, taking little steps with your feet so that the board swings round as well. You then get into position for the new tack with the wind behind you and the rig to leeward, and get under way once again.

As self confidence and skill increase, you can speed up this manoeuvre, turning the board by inclining the rig aft, and moving round the *front* of the mast. As the nose of the board passes through the eye of the wind, you catch the wishbone on the new side, rake the rig forward, sheet in, and head off on the new tack, taking it easy all the time. You will find you get faster and your technique gets better.

Next rake the rig forward, and transfer your new back hand to the boom (**6**). Grab it with your new front hand (**7**), and then sheet in and sail off on the new tack (**8**).

You can use exactly the same technique for learning to tack slowly in light winds. Keep your body upright and in balance, and when you get to positions **4** and **5** swing the boom end round the tail of the board which will turn it onto the right course for the new tack, ready for you to get hold of the boom and sail away.

If you have a mast track it may be easiest if you slide the mast to the back, leaving room in front.

Gybing

Gybing is the opposite of tacking. Rather than the nose of the board passing through the eye of the wind, it is the stern that passes through it, with the wind behind the board. Like tacking, gybing is a matter of technique – but there are even more variations. In its simplest form – shown on this page – it is one of the easiest manoeuvres to execute.

Basic Gybe

The basic gybe is the mast gybe. You sail on a dead run, and then incline the rig well to windward so that the board bears away. As the stern passes through the eye of the wind, transfer your hands to the mast (sheet hand before mast hand). Let the rig swing round and then grab the wishbone on the new side with your new sheet hand and mast hand.

A stronger wind will speed up the process of turning so that the board changes direction a great deal more quickly and dramatically.

1 Sailing on a run with the wind behind you, bear away by inclining the rig to the windward side of the board.

2/3 As the tail of the board passes through the eye of the wind, let go with the back hand, transfer it to the mast, and let the rig pivot round.

4/5 Grab the boom on the new side with the old front hand.

6 Sheet in and sail off.

If the wind isn't strong enough, you may need to shove the rig round which will also help turn the board.

Clew First Gybe

The clew first gybe looks very neat.
1 Start off on a run.
2 Begin to incline the rig well to windward.
3 If it's windy you may be travelling fast, so you need to slow the board down. To do so, step back so that the stern begins to drag in the water.
4 You can steer the board through the gybe by pushing down the windward side. On a roundboard this will make the board turn much faster.
5 Carry on turning the board so that the stern passes through the eye of the wind and you have turned so far that the clew of the sail is facing into the direction the wind is coming from.
6 Transfer your sheet hand to the mast. The rig will whip round to a broad-reaching position, so that you can reach out with your new sheet hand and sail away without losing speed throughout the entire manoeuvre.

Sailing clew first keeps on power which keeps the board turning throughout the gybe. A variation is the flare gybe, in which you jump back and sink the tail, lifting most of the board out of the water so that it can pivot round onto the new course as you steer it with the rig. In the second half of this book you can read about carve gybes at planing speeds.

Safety

Windsurfing can be dangerous unless you follow basic rules which make it safe – otherwise you'll risk drowning yourself and giving the sport a bad name. Here are the most important rules:

1. Don't go off sailing in a strong offshore wind unless there is assistance to hand. Unless you have requested help (should you need it) before setting off, you should never need to be rescued. Don't be the cause of a major air-sea rescue search – it costs the taxpayer a lot of money and it wastes a lot of time.

2. Check out the weather forecast carefully before you leave. If strong winds are forecast, take heed, and act accordingly.

3. Check out tides and other dangers. If you're in a warm country, you don't want to step on a sea urchin. Worse still, you don't want a shark to mistake the bottom of your board for some nice soft white underbelly.

4. Be very careful of the cold. It catches up on you faster than you think, so dress up, not down. In most circumstances you should wear a wetsuit and footwear as a matter of course. If it's really cold, you can wear a dry suit, but be very careful. You can't swim well in it, and if you lose your board you'll just have to bob up and down like the Michelin man.

5. Can you swim? You shouldn't be going windsurfing in the first place if you can't. If you have any doubts about your ability to cope with the conditions, wear a buoyancy aid.

6. Check every detail of your board. Is anything likely to break? You'll be really stuck if the mast foot gives out. Carry a towline which you can also use as a replacement if the outhaul or inhaul lines break – the neatest way is to carry it wound tightly around the after end of the wishbone.

If you're going to use a harness, always carry spare harness lines as well.

You must leash the mast foot to the board. If you have a bad fall, and the board, the rig, and you part company, you'll have a major problem getting it all back together again.

7. Learn the right of way rules. You need to know who has right of way, but don't push your luck. The other sailor might not be so well clued up, and you should make every effort to avoid a collision even if you are in the right.

8. Keep out of the way of shipping. Narrow channels and shipping should be avoided at all costs. Ships can't stop or alter course – if you mess them about you deserve to be banned from the water.

9. Avoid swimmers. They have as much right to the water as you do, and they aren't so manoeuvrable. A board can accelerate to ten or 15 knots pretty easily, and that's quite fast enough to kill your first swimmer!

10. Never abandon your board. It will continue floating long after you can, and it can be paddled for longer than you can swim.

11. Learn the International Distress Signals. Then at least someone will know you're drowning and not just waving.

12. Don't go out at night or in the fog. It's a very good way to get lost – two Swedish windsurfers went one better and got lost for good that way. Remember also that sharks come out for dinner when it's dark.

13. If you go out alone, tell someone what you're up to. It's OK to go out alone if you're sure you can handle it, but tell someone what you're up to just in case things go wrong.

14. Learn self-help techniques before you need them. You should find out just how easy it is to stow the rig and paddle the board. Different boards have different requirements – you should also find out what it's like being towed behind a motor boat.

15. Recognize hypothermia. Hypothermia is the condition when you start to get cold (just shivering) and then carry on getting colder. The final stages are unconsciousness followed by drowning, and in northern waters it doesn't take long to get to them.

Not only do you get cold when you're hypothermic, but you also get weak and apathetic. The process becomes a vicious circle of falling off your board and getting colder and weaker, so that you fall off the board again and again and again. . . .

For a windsurfer, the answer is to come ashore as soon as you start to feel cold and tired. If you can, have a hot shower, and get into some warm clothes as soon as possible.

If you decide to stay out on the water, then you're looking for trouble. If you're stuck out there and can't get back, then you're in trouble.

If you're on the board, you must try and keep the blood circulation going while you're battling against the *chill factor* induced by the wind – you've got to keep warm and paddle the board towards help.

If you're in the water, don't leave the board and swim unless it's clearly the best answer. Water conducts heat away from the body 26 times faster than still air, and if you can keep your head above the water, you should go into the HELP huddle, with your legs tightly crossed and your arms wrapped round your body.

16. Choose the right sail area. There's no point in going out if you can't handle the conditions with the rig you've got. A board with a small rig that is in control will go much faster than one with a bigger rig that is out of control – and it will get you home as well.

This is Baron Arnaud de Rosnay attempting to windsurf the English Channel for a wager, and being rescued for his pains. He left his board behind, and no one knows who claimed it.

Self-Help

In some circumstances you will have to pack up the rig and paddle home – either if something breaks, or if you're inexperienced and can't handle the conditions.

Sit down on the board facing the direction the wind is coming from; then take out the mast foot and undo the leash. Push the rig away from the mast first, so that the board blows downwind away from it. You can then undo the outhaul, and, starting at the clew, roll the sail up tightly until you get to the mast. Then lash the end of the wishbone near the top of the mast with the outhaul line, wrapping it around as much of the sail as possible at the same time. You should do the same with the uphaul at the lower end of the mast.

You can then put the stowed rig on the board, lashing it if possible so that it doesn't get dislodged by the waves.

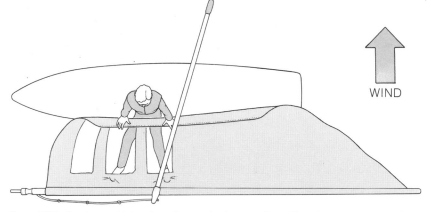

WIND

Top: With the board blowing downwind away from the rig, you can undo the outhaul and roll the sail from the clew with the battens removed. It should be a tight roll at the mast, which can then be lashed with the uphaul line and outhaul line, with the wishbone tied alongside.

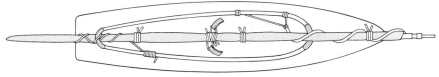

Above: You can then put the whole rig on the board, with the mast foot facing forward. If you can, lash it so it won't slide off the board when you are paddling. If you are in real trouble, don't have any compunction about leaving the rig behind if you need to.

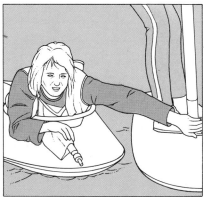

The best way to paddle is by lying on the board (above left). Alternatively you can kneel or sit astride it. If you can find someone to give you a tow, you can grab hold of his mast foot and lie alongside (above right), keeping the boards as close together as possible.

You will find both techniques surprisingly difficult. It is best to find out just how difficult before you need to use them in earnest, when there won't be time for any mistakes – it's a long hard struggle getting back upwind like this when it's blowing hard.

The international distress signal (left) is to wave your arms slowly back and forth over your head. You must use it so people appreciate you are not just waving.

Paddling
You can either lie or kneel on the board, paddling it with your hands. It is generally easier with the daggerboard retracted. If things look really grim, you should have no compunction about abandoning the rig, which will be greatly hindering your progress. If you have been sensible, it will have been insured, so it can be replaced.

You'll need to be careful not to get broadside on to waves, which will roll over both board and rig.

Flares
If you're sailing alone in rough water, carrying flares is a sensible precaution. You can get small packs of flares specially designed for windsurfing. You can carry them strapped to your leg, or in a harness pack, or in a sail pocket.

Lifejackets
A lifejacket supports the head above water – a buoyancy aid does not.

Most lifejackets are far too bulky for windsurfing, but in some cases it may be worth sailing with a CO_2/orally inflated lifejacket that can be combined with a harness and won't constrict movement or get in the way.

Reefing
If the wind blows up and catches you out, it would be ideal to be able to reef the sail as you can on a yacht. Sailmakers have tried out various ideas with zips etc, but unfortunately none have worked very well.

There are two ways of reefing a conventional windsurfing sail. Either you can take it off the mast

Expert conditions! With the right equipment an expert can sail in very strong winds and mountainous waves. However it takes considerable expertise.

and re-rig it without the bottom panels beneath the wishbone – somehow you'll have to roll them up into a neat bundle. Alternatively, you can attempt to roll the top half of the sail round the mast with the outhaul and downhaul slackened. Neither method works well, and it is much better to use a sensible size rig, keep close to the shore, and not go beyond your capabilities.

Even if you have a reefable sail, you are likely to be blown out to sea before you complete reefing it, which is a difficult operation in strong winds on the water.

Handling Stronger Winds

When the wind is light and the sea is flat, most people can master windsurfing in a few days. As long as you have enough balancing ability to ride a bicycle, and understand what the rig is doing, there should be no problems.

However, this type of windsurfing is fine in hot weather if you've nothing better to do. Otherwise it can be a little boring, particularly when you see the speeds at which other windsurfers travel when it blows hard. As the lift from their sails is combined with a light board/body weight, they are planing while you are displacement sailing. This means that your board is sailing through the water and its speed is governed by its length, while theirs is skimming over the water having broken through the displacement barrier.

When a board starts to plane, the proportional increase in speed is enormous, and so is the fun. To counter the force of the wind you must lean back with your body close to the water, while the board hisses and dances beneath your feet, with a shower of spray on each side. When you've done it once, you're hooked.

The Problems
Because it displaces so little wetted area, an Open Class roundboard will start to plane very easily – in Force 2 with a skilled sailor. The flat board is pushing more water, and consequently takes more wind to break free and plane – say Force 3 or 4.

This is the wind speed barrier that you need to surmount, and you will find it more difficult than mastering the initial stages of windsurfing. It is the barrier where some people give up.
1. The wind
When the wind is less than Force 2, there is little pull in the sail. You can control the rig as you want it.

As the wind speed increases the rig will pull harder, and when it

Above: Jumping demands a high level of fitness, combined with first-class technique.

starts getting on for Force 4, the problems will start.

Everything happens so much quicker. You can't pull the rig up out of the water, as the wind pressure is holding it down, and with several gallons of water trapped in the sail and its sleeve, you seem to be pulling up an immense weight. Your strength is sapped, and when you get it up, you find you cannot counter the force of the wind – the rig is blown from your hands by a gust, or worse still you hang on and it takes you with it.
2. The waves
When there is wind, there are likely to be waves. If you're sailing in a strong wind on the sea and there aren't any waves, it means that you are sailing off a weather shore and are very likely to get blown out to sea. The onshore wind is safe, but with surf breaking on the shoreline and the board being thrown everywhere, how do you stay on your feet?

Inshore waters won't have such big waves. The smaller and less exposed the area, the smaller you

will find the waves – but then you'll be plagued by a gusty wind caused by the obstructions on shore.

Either way you have the problem of controlling increased pressure in the sail, with a very unstable board beneath your feet, a fitful and gusty wind, or both.
3. Strength
The reason many people give up windsurfing at this stage is that they believe they are not strong enough.

Lifting the rig, controlling it, falling off the board and attempting to get going again, all seem to sap an inordinate amount of energy – particularly when sailing in a cold climate.

The Answers
Through lack of knowledge you make it harder for yourself. Strong winds are handled by *technique* and *equipment*, and though strength is important, Force 4 sailing can be enjoyed by anyone of average physical fitness. As the wind increases, so must your technique improve – only extreme conditions will demand unusual strength.

There are three main rules for strong wind sailing. Once you master them, you master your board:
1. Understand the theory
You must know why the board and rig are behaving the way they are.
2. Master the technique
You cannot hope to fight wind and waves on equal terms. You must learn when and how to give in to them, so that they can be exploited to best advantage.
3. Use the right equipment
'I can't lift the rig' may mean lack of strength or technique, but it may simply be solved by putting on a smaller sail. The harsher the conditions, the easier the board must be to sail.

Right: Keeping control in strong winds can be difficult, and it doesn't help if there is surf breaking under your board.

Suitable Boards

Generally speaking, the most suitable board for strong winds is one with the nomenclature 'funboard'. This can range from a long all-round-funboard which has relatively high volume (around 200 litres), down to short board sinkers with as little volume as 60 litres.

No board can be good in all conditions, and the more suitable a board is for strong winds, the less suitable it will be for light winds. A typical allround-funboard is slow and a little frustrating in Force 2; is very fast and great fun in Force 3–5; and becomes difficult to sail in Force 6. The extreme board such as the sinker is only usable in winds over Force 6!

Typical funboard characteristics

Below: Early funboard designs had square tails with a lot of volume. The pintail is now more usual.

Bottom shapes

The funboard shape is basically flat for stability. It is slow in light winds, and is at its best when the board is planing, skimming over the top of the water. Funboard design refinements include single and double concave bottom shapes. The double concave creates a V in the centre for directional stability, while the concaves are said to accelerate the water down either side of the hull which makes the board start planing quicker. Note the lift in the nose ('rocker') which prevents it diving through waves.

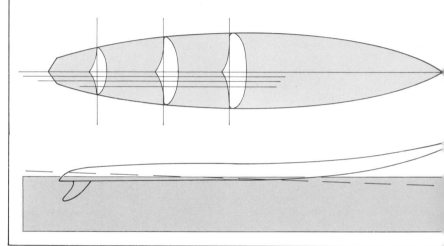

Volume

The volume of a board is equal to its flotation and is a good guide to suitability. When calculating your body weight, you should allow for wet clothing which may add another 10 kg. Reading along the body weight and volume lines you will see that a 70 kg beginner really needs a board of around 220 litres.

A board with any less volume will seem too unstable, but with more experience it will be more than enough volume.

The amount of volume is not the only consideration. Its distribution, and the length and width of the board will also affect performance and stability.

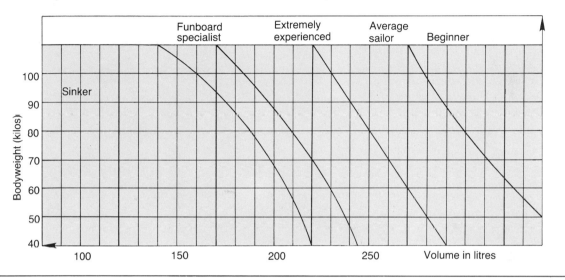

are a rather flat, stable bottom shape which is designed to be most effective when planing; a rounded pintail outline which is shaped so it can 'carve' gybes; and footstraps.

An allround-funboard is likely to be fitted with a fairly small fully retracting daggerboard; and a sliding mast track to trim the board for optimum performance. Construction of the board needs to be strong.

Any boards can be sailed in strong winds, but a funboard will be much the most *user friendly*. A Division II roundboard becomes very unstable and difficult to control, while the standard of fittings and rig on a basic flatboard are likely to be unsuitable for enjoying much more than Force 4.

Right: A flat, stable board such as the Windsurfer performs well in stronger winds, but is more demanding on technique.

Rigs and Sails

Just as a yacht reefs its sails as the wind blows harder, so a windsurfer must change to a more manageable size of sail.

From this point of view windsurfing is not a cheap sport. The strong wind enthusiast will need three or more sails specifically for the job. As a rough guide, the size of sail you use depends on your ability and weight (a big sailor carries a bigger sail), as well as on the conditions.

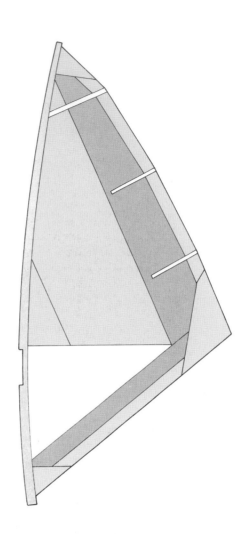

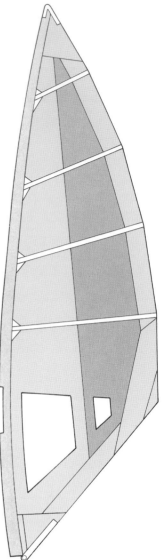

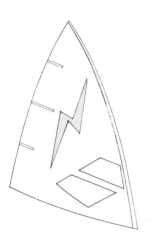

The IYRU Open Class regatta sail looks relatively old fashioned with triangular outline and a long boom of around 2.70 m.

A good design for a modern sail which can be used in strong winds. Note the vertical cut panels, the full length batten supporting the head, the large window for good vision, and the strong reinforcement at all three corners of the sail.

A more extreme high aspect modern design for use with a very short boom (1.70 m or less) on a very short board. The full length battens maintain stability.

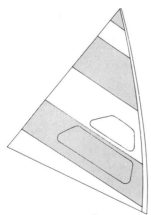

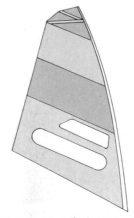

The basic cheap triangle is not likely to perform very well in anything except light winds.

The horizontal cut 'fathead' with horizontal cut panels – fashionable some years ago but now outdated.

Early strong wind sails had hollow leeches with no battens. Performance was not very good.

So, for medium to strong wind use (Force 4) you will need a sail of around 5.8 sq m, dropping to 5.2 sq m as the wind increases. For Force 6 and more 4.1 sq m would be about right, and for children or in really difficult conditions you could drop down to 3 sq m.

Unless you are triangle racing, a fibreglass mast is preferable. It is more resilient than alloy, and if it breaks in the surf it can often be repaired. If you can afford it you may find it worth buying a 'heavy duty' mast, some of which are guaranteed against breakage.

For stronger winds a short boom length with a fairly high clew is preferable. It makes the rig easier to pull up out of the water, and it is likely to make the centre of effort more stable and easier to control while you're sailing. A boom length of around 2.10 m is about normal for a 5.8 sq m sail, while smaller sails can have much shorter booms which are best suited to short boards under three metres.

Construction and Design

Most sails for stronger winds are at least partly supported by full length battens, with one or two supporting the head to give a 'powerhead' outline. Others which are more specialized have an elliptical outline supported by as many as eight full length battens.

Materials in current use are highly sophisticated and hard wearing. The more ordinary sail materials are polyester fibre (trade names include *Dacron* and *Terylene*); while the more exotic plastic film laminates (*Mylar*, *Melinex*, etc) claim superior performance characteristics, but are more expensive and don't appear so durable.

Hawaii is one of the leading centres for strong wind sail development, with breakthroughs that have included inventing 'rotational' sails in 1984.

Getting Going

The board should be very carefully prepared for sailing in stronger winds.

The mast step should be firmly in place. Most important of all – *the rig must be leashed to the hull*. If you wipe out, and the rig, board, and yourself become separated – you have problems. First you have to swim for the board, and if it's a light one it may be blown downwind faster than you can catch it. Then (hopefully) you have to paddle for the rig, which may have sunk in the meantime.

Make sure *all lashings on the rig are correctly done*: the outhaul, downhaul, and wishbone lashing. If the *non-slip finish is not good enough* (all over the board), apply some board wax, which you should be able to buy from a windsurf shop.

Conditions

Are they suitable? If there is an offshore wind, are you going to be able to get back? Are there any strong currents? How cold is the water? What's the weather forecast?

Windsurfers often ignore these questions, and then find that they

Right: The beach start is the neatest form of launching, but can only work if there is a cross wind. Slide the board into the water with one hand on the tail, and the other supporting the rig. When the water comes to your knees, drop the tail, and put both hands on the boom. Push on the mast foot until the board is on course for a broad reach, then step up with the back foot followed by the front foot and sail away.

Below: Wait for a break before launching in surf.

can't beat back through a gusty offshore wind that's increasing all the time. They fall into cold water with increasing regularity, as they become progressively less capable of handling the board. Then the tide turns and begins to sweep them down the coast – with luck they get rescued and simply cause a lot of trouble to everyone else.

1. Check that conditions are suitable.
2. Check the weather.
3. Don't use a sail that's too big.
4. Wear the right clothing.
5. Check the board thoroughly.
6. Let someone know what you're up to before you leave.

Getting on the Water

If the water is relatively flat, you can launch in the normal way.

If there is any surf, you must pull your board out through the

Right: The water start is another way of getting going. With your feet on the side of the board, you wait for the wind in the rig to lift you out.

83

breaking water, and hopefully find a flat spot between the waves where you can hop on quickly and get going. If the wind is blowing across your launch place, you can go for the nifty 'beach start', which looks good to spectators, and is not as difficult as you would imagine. The sequence is on page 82, and the main point to remember is to keep the board beam on to the wind, and not let it round up.

Getting Under Way

Getting under way in strong winds gets progressively more difficult as the wind speed increases.

If there are any waves, you've got a problem staying on the board, let alone sailing it – but even on flat water it's tricky.

Think out the problems first. There is much more force in the sail, and therefore a more powerful CE. This means that whereas the board would sail in a straight line in lighter winds, the CE is now pushing harder so that the board is constantly rounding up into the wind.

You can solve this problem by technique or equipment – it will probably be a combination of both:

1. Equipment
On pages 78–79 we looked at suitable strong wind boards, which have footstraps, small retracting daggerboards, and sliding mast tracks which are all designed to make handling easier in Force 4+ conditions.

On pages 80–81 we looked at rigs and sails, where the trend is to have a shorter boom with the CE well forward in the sail.

Boards and rigs specifically designed for strong wind use will have some or all of these features in various combinations, while basic learner boards can be adapted with minor changes of detail – for instance with a smaller rig and storm daggerboard, an old secondhand Windsurfer becomes an easy board to sail in strong winds.

2. Technique
When sailing in stronger winds you hang beneath the rig, so that it supports your weight. The reasons for this are:

1. The more a yacht heels, the less heeling effect the wind has on its sails – to be able to cope with the

Above: Footstraps make the allround-funboard easier to sail when the going gets rough. Below: On the Division II board there are no footstraps, and it's sometimes difficult to keep your feet on the board with breaking waves and the rig pulling hard.

strength of the wind, you must heel your rig on a windsurfer.

2. The rig lifts the board. In effect it makes it lighter, so that it planes more easily and goes considerably faster.

Getting Under Way by Numbers

Getting the rig up out of the water is your first problem. The wind catches it when it is still very full of water, so with the mast tip a few inches clear of the surface, you must wait until the board slews round into the wind, which will get under the rig, and help lift it for you. You can then rapidly haul it clear, back it to get to the wind abeam position, and stand by to take off.

If it's rough, you've got to get going straight away – if the water is flat you can take your time.

Bearing in mind the problems with your CE, you must be prepared to grasp the wishbone considerably further back than you have been used to – you can then rake the mast to windward until it touches your shoulder. The sheet hand then sheets in gradually, while you let your weight fall back to be supported by the sail. If the board begins to luff, cant the rig sharply to windward, sheet in, and if necessary push the front of the board away with your foot.

Once you can prevent the board from luffing, you have mastered the art of getting under way in strong winds.

Sailing Upwind

Beating has similar problems to 'getting under way' – for example, the board always wants to luff. Even boards that are specifically set up for strong winds can have this problem, as most of them are designed primarily for reaching.

The trick is to always keep the rig raked forward, and counter the gusts by raking it further forward still, while playing the sheet hand to feather the sail.

To point high, you need a large daggerboard, but you can sail fast and free with a smaller daggerboard (or if it's very windy, skegs alone) without the problems of railing or luffing.

Be wary of lulls. When the wind drops suddenly, the trick is to do a knees bend and bring your weight inboard rapidly.

In strong winds a retracting daggerboard makes control much easier; if you're going fast enough it can even be retracted upwind. Some older boards such as the Windsurfer were fitted with daggerboards which went straight up or down. This sailor has pulled the dagger up a few inches to make the board easier to control.

Falls

Getting going in stronger winds is difficult enough, but once under way, and even in relatively flat water, one's first impression may be that the board is behaving in a temperamental manner.

Catapult Falls

Once you have got started in stronger winds, the catapult fall is liable to be your first major problem. Sailing along happily on a reach, or bearing away, a gust hits the rig and the sailor strains to keep his balance and hold the wishbone. However the wind is too strong. He is plucked off his feet and vaulted into the rig, rather like going over the handlebars of a bicycle.

Of course. this can be fun for shore watchers, but it soon gets tiring, and if you are catapulted into the mast or the front of the board it can be expensive and dangerous. A head is quite capable of breaking a mast and the surface of the board is quite capable of breaking a head.

There are two alternatives:
1. Leave it!
It doesn't take long to know when you can't handle it. Another second and you will be lifted off your feet, so *let go!* In a light wind, letting go with the boom hand would have sufficed, but in this case let go with both hands – and abort gracefully backwards into the water. Nothing will be damaged, and you will have used considerably less strength than being swung through the air, and then having to retrieve the board and pick up the pieces.
2. Handle it!
As your technique improves, so should your need to 'Leave it!' diminish.

Like getting under way, success in averting a catapult fall depends on your ability to understand and handle the rig. When the gust comes, the sail must be feathered into the wind. The mast hand banks the rig to windward while the boom hand lets out the sail, spilling out the wind. It's a knack which you soon pick up, reacting in time with the wind.

Sometimes conditions are so unpredictable that you need more

On a flat board this will only tend to happen on reaches, when the board is going really fast. On a roundboard, due to its speed and a shape which encourages it to roll over, it will happen upwind as well.

There are two ways to deal with this problem:

1. Weight

As the board tips, shift your feet to the windward rail to push it down. Once back to normal, shift your weight inboard again.

On a roundboard with the mast foot pushing, you need to do this all the time. You may rake the daggerboard aft a little, but if you are racing you will need most of it down.

Therefore a very different technique – 'railing' – becomes necessary. These racing boards benefit from being sailed slightly on edge, since it increases their efficiency upwind. On this point, a roundboard is positively encouraged to sail on its side, while the sailor controls the amount of 'rail' with his feet on the windward edge, pushing down as the rail rides up too much, and letting it rise up if it's too far down. All the time he's doing knee bends to achieve this, with his torso held rigid by the harness line, sheeting the sail in and out as necessary.

However, most strong wind sailing is done on flatboards, and with these, capsize falls can be counteracted by:

2. The daggerboard

It is the daggerboard that is the main problem on a flatboard. Withdraw it, or cut down its area, and the problem is removed.

Therefore, if you are sailing for fun and the board is flipping up on its side, the answer is to retract the daggerboard. You will make more leeway, but if you're just enjoying yourself it doesn't matter. However if you're racing you must learn to sail upwind with the dagger down, and if you have a mast track slide the rig forward until the board feels comfortable.

Above and left: The catapult fall at its most dramatic. The sailor doesn't let go of the wishbone and is catapulted over the rig. This can pull the mast foot out of the board, so it is imperative that it is leashed. Special care should be taken when wearing a harness. If you don't unhook, cannonading into the mast could break it, or knock you out. Alternatively, if you end up with the rig on top of you, the harness line has a nasty habit of taking a couple of turns round the hook, and it becomes difficult to escape from under the water. A V-shaped hook will help prevent this, but it is always advisable to have a quick release buckle so that you can get the harness right off in a hurry.

than technique to stay on your board. Constant bucking and changes in speed over waves threatens to throw you off balance. It is then that the right choice of rig, and a board equipped with footstraps that anchor your feet against the gusts, extend your ability to sail into the most difficult weather.

Capsize Falls

The capsize fall is caused by the daggerboard – and your technique.

As the board gathers speed it begins to aquaplane on its daggerboard. It rises up like a hydrofoil until it balances precariously, with the thrust from the mast foot pushing the board over to leeward. Suddenly it will say 'No more!', and flip up and over on its side.

Reaching

The reaches are the best fun. The board really gets up and goes, and it's all spray and excitement.

Bearing Off

Bearing off from a beat to a reach requires a different technique, depending on what sort of board you are sailing.

On a flatboard you must steer it round with the rig. Rake it forward, sheet in (and out so you're not thrown off balance), crouch down a little for stability, and push with your front foot if necessary. That way the board will soon bear off, but beware the catapult fall!

If you have footstraps, it's a lot easier since your feet will be anchored against any sudden pull by the rig. Also, if you're going fast enough on an allround-funboard with a pintail outline, you can help turn the board by banking it like a ski. This is called 'carving' a turn, and becomes quite normal when you graduate to high speed funboard sailing on shorter boards. It's an exciting technique which demands a lot of practice.

Taking Off

Once on a reach you should take off. In any wind over Force 3 it's the fastest point of sailing – the wind is on the beam for maximum drive.

The daggerboard must be retracted, or the board will rail up on its side and become uncontrollable. (If your board doesn't have a retracting daggerboard, it will be worth investing in a shorter 'storm' daggerboard.)

If you have a mast track and are confident of maintaining control, you should pull the rig to the back of the track. With the dagger retracted the board should be perfectly balanced, and it enables you to hold the rig more upright so you can generate maximum power.

You can also make comfortable use of the footstraps, and the rule of thumb is that the faster you go, the further back you should stand in order to keep the skeg buried in the water. Select the straps which seem most comfortable, and keep the board moving fast without burying the tail.

NB. *When you fit footstraps, make sure they are the right size for your foot or boot. They should be just big*

enough to get a good grip, but not so big that your foot could slide through.

Weight Distribution

This is important on the reach. You must keep the nose of the board well up so it won't submarine when it accelerates, and keep it steering straight with your feet – on a round board you'll need to dance a constant jig to try to keep it level and

Reaching in moderate winds the sailor takes a comfortable stance, facing forward with his arms bent so he can see what's coming and guide the board over the waves. Standing too far back would bury the tail and slow the board, so keep forward until it starts to really get moving.

prevent it heading up or bearing off. The stronger it blows, the further outboard your feet need to be, but there comes a point when your heels dig in the water and send up a shower of spray, so you need to shift your feet inboard once again.

Bearing Off on to the Run
The technique is the same as for bearing off on to a reach – but it's

even less fun. At least on the reach the rig is pulling, but when going on to the run, there comes a horrible moment when the wind goes behind, and the sail stops sucking as the laminar flow ceases. If you continue to pull, you'll fall in, so transfer your weight inboard pretty smartly, and get behind the sail, standing two square in your new running stance.

Reaching at speed on a modern allround-funboard. Shorter funboards can change direction simply by 'footsteering'; weighting either side of the tail. A longer allround-funboard is not so responsive and will rely wholly or partly on steering with the rig. Note the short boom and high clew of the sail, which is well clear of the waves when the rig is pulled back.

Running

Running is the nightmare of all windsurfers.

With the wind right behind, you just can't lean back and enjoy yourself, but need to pursue a wobbly and precarious course, with no stability on either side.

In theory you need never run at all. You could close reach all the time (and never have to beat), but in reality there will come an occasion when you have to sail on a run or wobbly broad reach – perhaps due to being swept upwind by the tide – and of course if you try Olympic triangle racing, you'll have to do it all the time.

The technique is similar to running in light weather, except that now the rig is pulling a lot harder, and things are happening a great deal faster. You can't see the gusts (or the competitors) coming up behind you, but you need to be on your guard, ready to hop to the back of the board, pulling at the rig with all your might.

Whether it's flat or round, the board will be very prone to steer according to its shape, shooting off in one direction or the other rather more rapidly than you would like. Either way you may fall in, or collide with another board.

Enemies

There are two major enemies. The first is:

The daggerboard

From down there in the depths, the daggerboard will decide to take control of your board as soon as you turn on to a run.

In most cases you should retract it fully, though you can try experimenting with a little down which may add stability. Once you have worked out where it should be, the second enemy will be:

Waves

Running through waves can be an

The only time short funboards sail on a run is during a gybe. For a couple of seconds they sail dead downwind as the board carves round onto the new reach. During this time they rely on momentum.

extremely unpleasant experience. Strangely enough, it's better if the wind is reasonably strong, as this at least gives you something to brace yourself against. If it is fitful, you don't know where you are and soon become prone to the most terrible wobbles.

If you can't handle it, you must try getting your weight lower and consequently rocking the boat less. (Some of the Division II racing boards tried a hollowed-out canoe-style hull, so that the sailor could get his weight lower.) Try going down on one knee, with the other leg spreadeagled behind you. It's uncomfortable, but it may work, and at least in this stance you can jump to your feet fairly rapidly.

If that's no good, try sitting down on the back end of the board,

with the rig pulled down over your head. You'll get your weight very low for stability, and cut the amount of sail exposed to the wind, but will be a little stuck for steerage. If rocking the rig from side to side doesn't have a quick enough effect, you can always drop a leg over the side to slow the board down and slew it round.

Sitting will get you downwind, although it might be a rather slow passage. However, whichever way you do it, don't fall off! It's a hell of a job getting going again, as you've got to find your board, gingerly raise the rig and then try and bear it away on the direction of a broad reach before starting off and getting back on to the run. This is fine for superhuman windsurfers, but for the rest of us, it takes a long time.

Gybing

Surprisingly, gybing is nothing like as difficult as running – perhaps it's the realization that you're getting off the run!

If you have steady nerves, you can gybe with the board running fast – if you haven't, you can always slow it down by standing on the back end so that the stern digs in and begins to drag.

You push the rig over to windward, crouching down with a little pumping of the sheet hand for stability. Pushing down on the windward rail the board will turn fast, but don't do anything until you are well through the eye of the wind – just right for a broad reach on the other tack. At this point, grab the mast just below the wishbone with your sheet hand. Take your mast hand off, the rig flips round, and hey presto, you can grab the new windward wishbone.

There are many variations on the strong wind gybe. Most of them relate to short funboards which are much more responsive and easier to control for this kind of sailing, but you have to be a good sailor and master their basic techniques first. You can read more about them on pages 114–125.

If All Else Fails

Getting downwind on a tippy round board can be a real problem. Unless you have got the knack of steering the thing with your feet, you'll be falling off every other minute and getting increasingly tired and unhappy. There is one very slow but effective option. Simply let the rig blow in front of you like a flag, and with luck it will bring you home. If you can't manage that, you'd better ask for a lift – ask any windsurfer and he will tell you that ignominy is the better part of valour when there's tea waiting at home.

Above: Standing on the back of a board, lifting its whole length clear of the water prior to a gybe. The photo shows an early square tailed funboard (1980 vintage) which will run straight, but be difficult to turn.

Right: In very difficult conditions Division II racers resort to lying on their boards.

The Harness

It was the Hawaiians, led by Larry Stanley, who invented the harness in the mid seventies, and if they had patented it they would have made a fortune. As it is, windsurfers have a lot to be thankful for. Whereas the sport used to depend largely on strength – roughly translated into how long you could bear to hang on for – you can now hook in, hang on, and go for miles.

This is because your back is taking the strain from the sail, rather than your arms which now simply control which way the rig is pointing.

Technique

Before you use a harness you should be a proficient sailor in strong winds – otherwise, what would you do if your harness or harness lines broke when you were out sailing? Also you still need some muscle, and it is good to develop your forearms by using a harness as little as possible when it is not blowing so hard.

The harness lines should be pre-stretched Terylene of around 5 mm diameter. They should be no more than 130 mm long, depending on whether you prefer them long or short.

You can simply tie them to the boom, or use custom-made tabs to hold the ends in place. Either way, they should only move when you want them to.

Try using a harness on dry land first. You need to hook in on the middle of the harness line, which will be about equal to the CE of the sail. Your hands should fall near each end of the line.

Obviously, the lines will need adjusting according to wind conditions. If it is blowing harder, you will want to shift them back along the wishbone to find the new CE.

When you are out on a board,

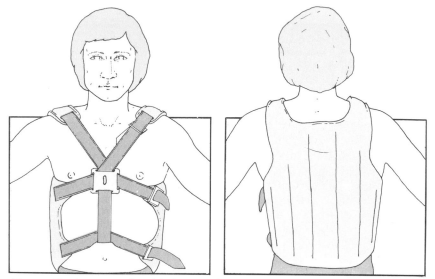

Above: The harness should give maximum support to the rib-cage, which is compressed, and the back from the shoulders to the waist. It should be a tight, but comfortable fit, with foam padding.

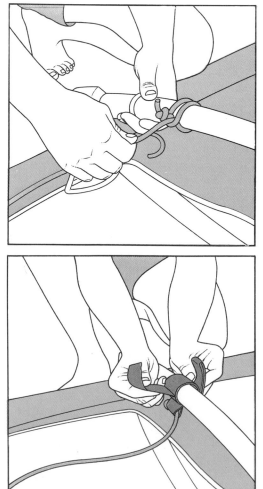

If you're on a budget you can buy 5 mm Terylene line and make your own harness lines cut to length. A figure-of-eight stopper knot secures each end, and they can be loosened and moved to different positions on the boom as necessary.

It's probably better to buy specially made harness lines which have webbing and Velcro attachments at each end. They are simple to use, and when the line wears through it can easily be replaced. Some also have a plastic buckle which makes adjustment easier.

The sailor dips his knees and pulls the wishbone towards him with a sharp jerk to swing the line . . .

. . . the hook catches, and he leans back to take his weight on the line, his hands on the wishbone.

there is a knack in getting used to a harness. Come on to a close reach, dip your knees, and at the same time pull the wishbone sharply towards you to flip the harness line into the hook.

Once you have got the hook in, lean back and take your weight on the harness . . . you'll find it's pure luxury!

You need to take care. If the rig pulls hard, you go with it, so you have to be aware of gusts, controlling the incidence of the rig with your hands, and sheeting out or banking it to windward as necessary. If you really can't control it,

you'll have to get unhooked or go with it.

The beats are relatively easy to predict and control when using a harness, but the reach is more difficult – if you catapult and you're hooked in, you can go head over heels and cause a lot of damage. On the run it is never wise to hook in, however tired you are.

If you come off when hooked on, the harness line has a nasty habit of taking a couple of turns round the hook. If you're under the sail and disorientated, getting unhooked can quickly become a frightening experience. A V-shaped hook is unlikely to tangle, but you should always wear a harness that has a quick release buckle so that you can take it off in a hurry if necessary.

Above: Perfect harness technique demonstrated by Ken Winner. His back takes the strain, while his hands control the rig, and his feet control the board. Note the very short harness lines – the length is quite adequate with a well balanced sail. If you find the harness compresses your chest, invest in a 'spreader bar' made of plastic or alloy, which is designed to spread the load.

A harness should give maximum support to the whole of your back and rib cage. It should be well padded, and either have a back pack or a pocket for carrying spare harness lines. Ideally it should have buoyancy, though few are designed to float you face upwards.

Getting Fit

To enjoy your windsurfing to the full it is worth making the effort to get fit for the job. Windsurfing is in in itself marvellous exercise, and the more you do the fitter you will become, but as with skiing you should try to get in reasonable shape for your board in the first place.

Cold weather saps energy very quickly in a strong wind. Before considering how to improve your muscles, you should look at two points:

1. Diet
The heavier you are the more weight you and your board have to carry. You get more tired than someone who is lighter, and your board travels more slowly. Therefore, watch your weight!

However, you need immediate energy and to this end sugar is your most effective form of nourishment. Make sure you eat properly before sailing, and if you are going out for a long time take some glucose tablets or even chocolate in your back pack.

2. Clothing
There is always the danger that your body will get progressively colder while you are out on the water. When you are sailing along in a strong breeze, you are using enough energy and pumping enough blood to keep warm, but once you stop, the cold sets in and you become less able to cope with the conditions.

You may be waiting for the start of a race, with the cold wind cutting down your body temperature, or you may fall off into cold water. Either way you must start exercising to keep the blood going. If you are unable to sail, sit on the board and do any exercise you can – twisting the body, shaking the wrists, and waving your arms like windmills over your head.

Strengthening the hands for the wishbone. Simply try to pull your clasped hands apart.

Strengthening hands. Squeezing a tennis ball is remarkably effective – and tiring!

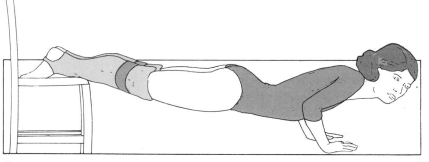
Strengthening arms and back. Press-ups are a particularly effective form of torture.

Strengthening arms and back. Push hard in a doorway, and try to emulate Samson.

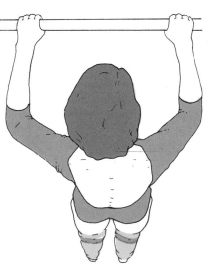
Strengthening arms and back. Pull-ups on a bar. Test the structure before you start.

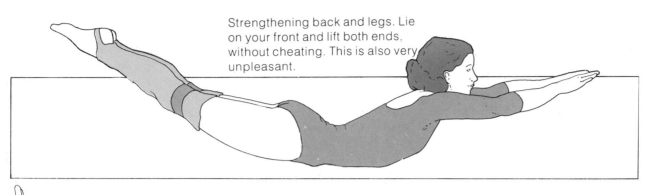

Strengthening back and legs. Lie on your front and lift both ends, without cheating. This is also very unpleasant.

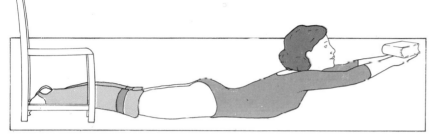

Strengthening back and arms. Don't lift your legs or you'll send the chair flying. Just try to lift your front half.

Strengthening back and legs. This one is not so difficult, but of course not as effective. It's the nasty ones that count.

Strengthening arms, back and legs. Raise your legs and stretch out your arms to meet them. This ends your daily routine.

So, be very careful about your clothing. It must keep you warm, but without promoting cramp by constricting your forearms.

Exercising

When you start windsurfing, most of your strength loss is in your hands and forearms. Until you have mastered harness technique (pages 92–93) the hands continuously clasp the wishbone, while the forearms carry the full weight of your body – the heavier you are, the stronger they must be.

The thighs, legs, and feet come under greater strain as your windsurfing becomes more advanced. Both roundboards and footstraps allow the sailor to control the direction of the board with his body rather than with the rig. With the roundboard he will constantly need to control the angle of rail with his legs – with footstraps his feet twist, push, and pull in the straps to steer the board.

You will benefit from visiting a gymnasium. Weightlifting strengthens the arms and the back, while bicycle machines and exercises will strengthen you from the waist down. Serious swimming is also very beneficial, but if you would rather make do at home, the exercises on these pages will help. These exercises should be done an increasing number of times each day. They are intended for both sexes and all ages, but if you're still not sure if you qualify, it may be wise to check with your doctor.

Top Techniques

When it comes to advanced techniques, the top champions will always be best. All day and every day they sail in the best places with the latest in boards and equipment to maintain their expertise.

However, given time and practice, any windsurfer can learn their techniques, whether they relate to racing in a World Championship, jumping in the waters off Hawaii, or designing and building a board from a foam core.

Regatta Sailing

To succeed as a regatta sailor requires dedication, and the international standard is so high that anyone aiming to become a World, European, or Olympic champion almost certainly needs to have a job connected with windsurfing (or wealth!). Only that way can he get the necessary time, expenses, and equipment to spend all the time training, racing, and travelling. Few sailors have become rich by windsurfing, but quite a few make a good living from it.

The single greatest problem for the regatta sailor is likely to be stress, which particularly affects younger, less experienced sailors. They can win a single race through instinctive ability, but it takes self-discipline and a cool temperament to have steady, high placings throughout a series, and in the end that's what counts the most.

The Racing Classes

The IYRU (International Yacht Racing Union), which is the governing body of international yachting competition, organises all major windsurfing competition with the exception of funboard racing which is dealt with in the next chapter.

The IYRU administer racing for the three 'Open Class' divisions and the international one-designs:

Open Class Division I
Series boards and prototypes with an absolute maximum hull thickness of 16.5 cm.

Open Class Division II
Production and prototype round boards with a maximum hull thickness of 22 cm. The Olympic class.

Open Class Division III
Tandems. All three classes use the same 6.3 sq m Open Class rig.

Windglider
The 1984 Olympic one-design, but outdated and now out of production.

Windsurfer
The biggest one-design in the world and the great 'original' design by Hoyle Schweitzer. Still a popular choice for racing.

Mistral
Based on the Mistral Competition, Light and Superlight designs. These boards were replaced by a completely new design (Competition SST) in 1985.

On a national level racing for the international classes is administered by national authorities such as the RYA and UKBSA in the UK.

Triangle Racing

Triangle racing is the norm for all of these classes.

Left: A race for an Open Class World Championship. This is one of the beats on the Olympic triangle, and as you can see the boards soon become very spaced out so that no one has a clear idea who is in front until they converge on the mark. This kind of competition is excellent for improving technique on any kind of board.

Above: Going from a reach to a reach as the boards gybe round the mark during the same race. When a lot of boards converge on a mark at the same time, there is a great deal of place swopping. Many have their wind affected by the boards behind, and it frequently pays to keep well clear and sail round the outside unless you are well established close in.

The idea of the 'Olympic triangle' has been adapted from the dinghy classes. The start is always into the wind, with three equal length legs which are usually about 1–2 km.

The Olympic triangle gives equal importance to beating, reaching and running. For this reason it is not suitable for most funboards which are designed primarily for reaching. Classes such as the Mistral one-design tend to use modified triangular courses which dispense with a long run dead downwind, and concentrate on fast reaching legs with relatively little beating. One of their most popular course shapes is a W (two triangles) which involves a lot of mark rounding. Division II always uses the Olympic triangle.

Preparation

Preparation is vital for any kind of racing. In particular it's one way of handling the stress of a big regatta.

Starting Procedure

Before the first race of a regatta, the competitor should have full knowledge of the starting procedure and the course – as well as having studied the detailed sailing instructions which are issued to all the participants.

It is essential not to make any mistakes. Work out what is required so that you can't get confused, and make sure you know by heart every flag the starter boat is likely to fly: red for a starboard hand course; green for a port hand course; the 'Blue Peter' for five minutes to go; the race abandonment flag; the shortened course flag; the requirement to wear a life jacket – and many more.

It is also necessary to learn all the right-of-way rules and rule infringements. For example, a competitor who touches a buoy on his way round it must go round it again, avoiding all other boards, or he will be disqualified.

Similarly, if a competitor first touches another board and then acknowledges he is wrong, he can avoid disqualification by executing a 720 degree turn – turning his board twice round beneath his feet, and once again avoiding all other boards.

The Board

It is essential for the underside of the board to have a reasonably smooth finish. However it shouldn't be too smooth. You should aim for a mat finish which will allow a thin layer of water to adhere to it. This is advisable since friction is least when water flows past water.

Top: In the *Open Classes* all boards need to be scrutinized and measured before they can race in a major championship.

Above: Sails need to be carefully treated. These *Open Class* sails are dried out and carefully stored between every race.

A 400 grade wet-and-dry sandpaper will achieve the right result on a good surface, and will also get rid of wax and grease.

Daggerboard and Skeg

These should be prepared along the same principles as the hull. Particular care should be taken with a laminated ply daggerboard, since it will be prone to warping, swelling up, and distortion if it is incorrectly stored or not properly varnished or painted. Constant attention – sandpapering, filling, varnishing/paint-

ing – will be necessary to keep the leading edges in raceworthy condition.

Many Division 2 boards have a slot gasket to prevent water coming up through the daggerboard case. You should always check that this is working effectively, and is properly bonded in place. With constant use, it may need replacing several times a season.

Topsides

Grip on the deck of the board is very important in racing. Apart

from choosing footwear which has a suitable rubber compound, you can improve the non-slip properties by rubbing on special board wax. (Sex Wax is a well-known brand!)

The Rig
If there's a choice, choose the right rig for the conditions. With classes such as the Windsurfer you are stuck with the standard sail, but in the Open Class you can go as small as you like. If this enables you to get round the course without falling off, you'll probably get to the finish

before the guy who's fallen off half-a-dozen times with a big sail.

Remember that where there is a choice of sails you will probably be limited to a total of two for use throughout the regatta.

When you choose your sail, plan for the series – not just the one race.

Other Equipment
Some regatta organizers require that you wear buoyancy aids. Check this one out, or you could get disqualified. In most cases a buoyancy harness will suffice.

Above: Between races check that everything is right with your board in plenty of time. Don't leave anything to the last minute.

Finally, and most important, you need a stopwatch with a 10 minute countdown. There was a time when these were very expensive. However, the new generation of digital quartz watches are ideal for the purpose. They have multi-functions, are relatively cheap, and in most cases are sufficiently waterproof.

The Start

A race starts long before the starting gun is fired. So a competitor should not only be armed with theoretical and practical knowledge of the regatta he will be sailing, but must also find plenty of time to warm up and practise various manoeuvres. These will loosen the muscles, allowing maximum physical performance during the race, and preventing any likelihood of cramp, as well as awakening the sense of fine balance which is so important when sailing a round-board.

Getting out early brings many advantages. Wind and waves can be studied, and the tactical approach can be planned. Once the buoys are in position, there is also time to work out which is the best side of the course to sail up.

Another advantage of getting to the start line early is that the competitor can try out his tack for the first leg. (Remember that a stopwatch is indispensable!)

In many ways, the start is the most important part of the whole race. At no other time will the competitors be so densely concentrated in one area.

Start Signals

Make sure you understand the signals before you go out to the start line. These are: a preliminary signal ten minutes before the start; another signal five minutes before the start; a preparatory one minute signal; then the start. If the start is unruly, the Race Officer may introduce the One or Five Minute Rules to discipline the field. These rules forbid boards to cross the line from any direction within the allotted time, and may lead to disqualification – they must be learnt by heart!

The first thing to remember at the start is not to take any position on the line which restricts your

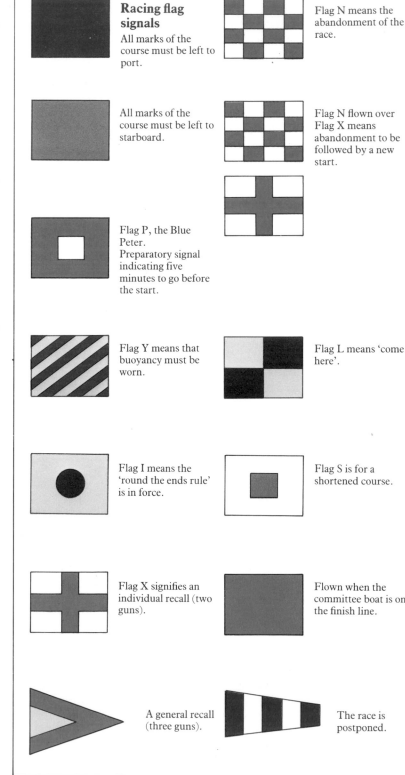

Racing flag signals

All marks of the course must be left to port.

All marks of the course must be left to starboard.

Flag P, the Blue Peter. Preparatory signal indicating five minutes to go before the start.

Flag Y means that buoyancy must be worn.

Flag I means the 'round the ends rule' is in force.

Flag X signifies an individual recall (two guns).

A general recall (three guns).

Flag N means the abandonment of the race.

Flag N flown over Flag X means abandonment to be followed by a new start.

Flag L means 'come here'.

Flag S is for a shortened course.

Flown when the committee boat is on the finish line.

The race is postponed.

freedom of movement (because of the other boards around you). You must be able to pump away fast. Thus:

1. You must be on the right part of the line with regard to the tactical requirements of the first leg.

2. You must cross the line with sufficient speed at the starting signal. This is only possible if there is enough space on your leeward side (2–4 m) to bear away and pick up speed. It can be done, however, by a competitor who knows the rules and keeps a cool head.

3. Go for speed first – the correct course comes second.

4. Lack of confidence may make you look back as you leave the line – and then you may as well go back to the start position!

In Conclusion

A good regatta surfer is one who possesses a high degree of concentration, who has strong nerves, and who has perfect control over the board. These factors are imperative in the chaos of the start line, as is a knowledge of the rules.

Start Positions

The choice of where to start depends on whether the start line is biased to the left or right hand side of the course, although the wind never blows constantly from any one direction. Even so, the sailor should try to decide which end of the line is nearest to the first mark. If there is no bias, it is probably best to start in the middle.

The Right Hand Side

Many competitors opt to start on the right hand side. As everyone wants to get the optimum windward placing, this approach will normally only succeed in very small regatta fields. It also becomes immensely difficult in a strong wind, when it is hard to keep the board in

Above: The bottom is scrupulously prepared before every race. This is a Division II board.

Below: When all the boards are the same make (Windsurfers here) mark which one is yours.

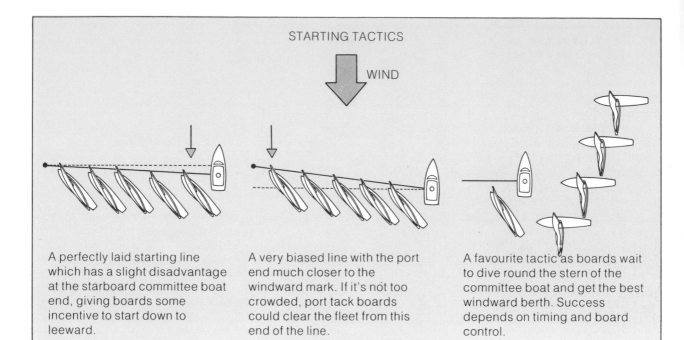

STARTING TACTICS

WIND

A perfectly laid starting line which has a slight disadvantage at the starboard committee boat end, giving boards some incentive to start down to leeward.

A very biased line with the port end much closer to the windward mark. If it's not too crowded, port tack boards could clear the fleet from this end of the line.

A favourite tactic as boards wait to dive round the stern of the committee boat and get the best windward berth. Success depends on timing and board control.

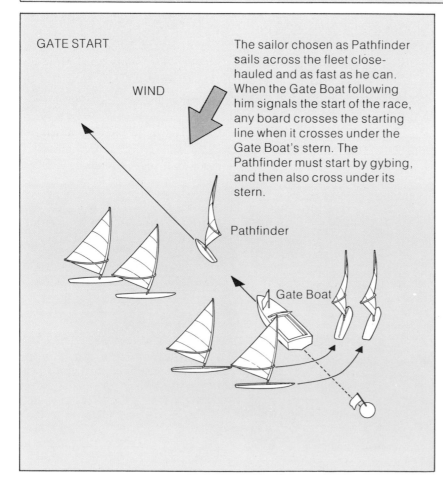

GATE START

WIND

The sailor chosen as Pathfinder sails across the fleet close-hauled and as fast as he can. When the Gate Boat following him signals the start of the race, any board crosses the starting line when it crosses under the Gate Boat's stern. The Pathfinder must start by gybing, and then also cross under its stern.

Pathfinder

Gate Boat

position – tucked in to windward of the fleet. You are always making leeway.

The best way to get the windward position is to sail round from behind the Committee Boat, and drift into position, at the same time killing the sail. This manoeuvre is very difficult and needs careful practice – remember that you have no right of way over other boards that are already on the line – just in the place you want!

You have to work out whether you want to be right up to windward – and hemmed in by all those wanting to be in the same position – or are better off starting a little further down to leeward so that you can sail free and fast.

If you have not succeeded in getting in the first line of boards, at least you have right of way over port hand boards.

The right hand side has many disadvantages. Even if it is the biased side of the course, so many sailors start there from habit and lack of imagination that you may get held up on your way to the first mark by their backwinding and everyone's lack of manoeuvrability. Those that cannot start at top speed soon get into a hopeless position, and fall back out of contention.

Therefore, unless it is immensely biased, try starting farther down to leeward on the line.

The Left Hand Side

Starting down this end, you need different tactics to get away at full speed. As this end normally has a small bias built in by the Committee Boat to compensate for the leeward position, you can get away immediately on the starboard tack, taking great care not to get pushed off the end of the line before it is time to start.

The initial reward in starting down at the port end of the line will be a free wind and room to manoeuvre – after that it will depend on whether the wind suddenly decides to head the boards on the starboard tack or free them, and you should have worked this out in your pre-regatta research.

Once you need to tack on to port, always make sure that there is a big gap in the starboard tack boards to make it worth your while.

Port Tack Start

To succeed with this start, the sailor must have enough room to cross the line at full speed at the port end of the line, and clear the mass of boards coming at him on the starboard tack. It demands precise timing and judgement, because if the starboard boards force him to tack, all may be lost.

Starting in the Middle

When you start in the middle, the boards on either side of you will determine your tactics. Luff the ones to windward, giving yourself enough room to leeward to bear off and hit the line at full speed. (Remember that on a long line there is always an immense sag, with boards two or three lengths behind the line.)

Above: If you are not sure about the performance of your board check it out with a friend.

Below: Many arrive at the start line late. It always pays to leave before the main rush.

The Race

Windward Legs

When you have left the start line, it is extremely important to choose the right initial tacks. Your tactics should be determined by your position relative to other boards and by wind shifts.

The overriding consideration as the start gun goes is to get clear so that you have total freedom of movement as to where you want to go. Boards to windward and to leeward cause adverse backwinding and get in your way – in this situation you must either free off and foot through to leeward, or tack if you can find a gap in the mass of boards sailing on the starboard tack. Once you're free of this massive interference from other boards, you are also free to choose your tacks.

In general, different tactics are demanded by inland waters and by the open sea. On inland waters you can expect constant wind shifts, which can make the greatest difference to victory or defeat. Therefore you must react instantly, by tacking on each wind shift. Only in this way will you make ground to windward at the fastest possible speed.

On the open sea it is rather different. There is usually a more constant wind, and speed differences between boards are far more likely to be influenced by sailing technique. The person who sails a board best through wind and waves sails fastest.

Of course, tactics also play their part. You should have precise knowledge of the tide – which way it is running and how fast. You should establish the likely weather pattern – will the offshore morning breeze turn onshore in the afternoon?

Sailing in waves demands great skill, particularly if the wind-blown waves are converging with the natural swell, which will result in a very confused sea. In this case you should always sail free and go for speed, particularly if you are getting into troughs that are so deep that there is no wind.

Rounding the Windward Mark

Choosing the final beat up to the buoy is critical. The most common mistake is to tack too soon. The closer you get, the more you have to pinch up to windward, and the board loses power and speed. If there are other boards converging on the mark ahead of you, their turbulence will begin to affect your performance so that you are pointing five degrees below your desired course.

The result is that you find you cannot get round the mark, so that you need to put in another short tack. The closer you are to the mark, the more difficult this is because of the other boards. However, attempting to squeeze round the mark and accidentally hitting it should be avoided at all costs. You will have to round it again, avoiding all the other boards, and you will lose many places.

Therefore you should always choose your last beat when you are relatively close to the mark. You will be close enough to get it right ('overstanding' the mark so that you have to reach down on it also loses a lot of places). If you're on the port tack, you won't find a dense mass of starboard tack boards converging on the mark unless you are very close to it – and then you can ascertain whether the mark will be clear enough for you to round it on the port tack.

Reaches

If your course is not affected by waves or the tide, you should always aim to sail the direct course for the next mark.

Reaching through waves is a great experience which also gives a regatta sailor a big opportunity to

enlarge his lead. However pumping is a problem which often results in lengthy protest meetings and eventual disqualification. The IYRU dictum is that there should be no pumping on the upwind legs, but on the reaches you can pump up to a maximum of three times to promote planing and surfing.

The reaching course involves a lot of snaking, as all wind and wave fluctuations should be used to keep

top speed. It is always important to luff towards a wave, and then bear away and surf with it.

If you want to overtake other boards, you have to decide whether to overtake to windward or to leeward. You should always take into consideration how this will affect your position on rounding the mark – whether you will be inside or outside other boards.

You must also be very careful if you are sailing with the daggerboard withdrawn. Your board will be very prone to attack by boards with their daggerboards down, since they may be more manoeuvrable.

Runs
Many sailors underestimate the importance of runs, but there are tremendous opportunities to improve your position.

A fleet of one-design Mistral Superflights racing during their World Championship in Barbados. The Mistral and other classes sometimes race round a 'flattened' triangle which has less beating, no runs, and a lot more reaching. The idea is to make racing more fun, and at the same time less demanding on advanced techniques. It is particularly suitable for stronger winds.

Here, more than at any other time, the boards behind can interfere with the wind of the leaders, and everyone should try to keep their wind clear.

You must also choose whether to head straight for the mark, or to try downwind tacking. If the wind is light, you're better off taking the shortest course, but with Force 4+ you can try very broad reaches on a number of tacks – even though you sail further, the speed difference may compensate.

If it's extremely windy, and there are big waves, you'll find downwind tacking is at its most effective. Increased pressure on the sail makes it easier for you to keep your balance, and you benefit from surfing down the wave faces.

Finish

Tactics at the finish are crucial. You must watch and cover your opponents all the time, without being taken in by a sham move. Try not to get too closely involved with another board – it will almost certainly lead to loss of overall places.

Watch out for any bias on the finish line. Theoretically it will be at 90 degrees to the wind, but in practice this is seldom the case – and crossing the right end of the line may win you the race.

Protests

Races can be won off the course, and a complete understanding of the racing rules is vital.

Sooner or later you will be involved in a protest if you aim to take your racing seriously. If the sailor in the wrong absolves himself by executing a 720 degree turn that is fine, but otherwise you must protest, remembering:

1. You must tell the other sailor you intend to protest. Cry 'Protest!' or '720!' If he then absolves himself, well and good.
2. If he doesn't, look for witnesses who can support your case.

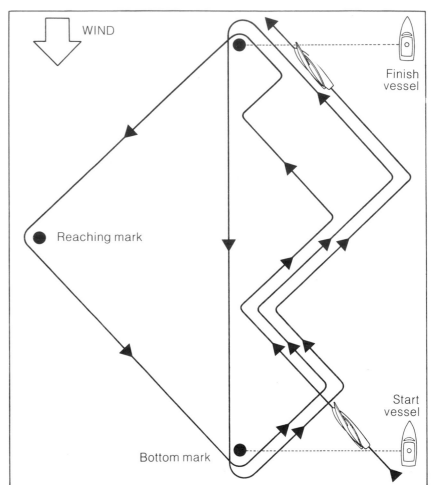

WIND

Finish vessel

Reaching mark

Start vessel

Bottom mark

3. Advise the committee boat.
4. When on land write down details and a diagram of your protest, quoting the relevant rule number. Deliver the protest to the race committee within the time limit.
5. Discuss the incident with your witnesses before they appear before the race committee.

If you are protested:
1. If you know you are in the wrong, avoid being disqualified with a 720.
2. If you reckon you are in the right, look out for witnesses.
3. Check that the protesting boardsailor has followed the correct procedure.
4. Check the relevant racing rule and prepare your defence with help from witnesses.

The Olympic triangle is used in most major regattas, and always works along the same principles.

The course is either a starboard hand course, or a port hand course, denoted by a green or red flag flown by the committee boat. The one illustrated here is port hand – ie all the marks are to port.

The first leg is a beat directly into the wind. The boards then bear away on a reach to the reaching mark, where they gybe on to the opposite reach. They then round the bottom mark and beat up to the top once again.

The next leg is a dead run back down to the bottom mark. Finally they beat up to the finish which is close to the top mark (and can be confused with it).

Above: Windsurfer class boards during their 1979 World Championship in Greece.

When there are a large number of identical one-design boards in a race such as this, a 'gate' is sometimes used at the start. Rather than every individual jockeying for position, a single board sails across the fleet at full speed on one tack. Every other board has to sail round its stern on the other tack in order to start, guaranteeing that everyone starts equally.

Left: Gybing around the mark during the Open Class World Championship held in Israel in 1980. The sailor is Thomas Staltmaier, who won the heavyweight class on a Mistral M1.

Funboard Racing

As the name implies, funboard racing is for funboards, and that means it can only be held if the right wind and water conditions exist.

Funboard racing is very different from the regatta sailing covered in the previous chapter. It has evolved without the help or interference of the IYRU and national bodies, and consequently encourages a much more *laisser faire* attitude to competition – no limitations on sponsorship or professionalism, the fewest possible rules, and as much razzamatazz as possible!

WSMA Disciplines
The top league of funboard racing is the WSMA World Cup, which started when a dozen or so of the world's leading board and sail manufacturers decided to set up an international professional windsurfing circuit. The object was to promote their products, while at the same time promoting windsurfing to the general public; and the World Cup is now recognized as a major source of research and development in windsurfing.

The WSMA wrote the rules for their regattas, and these are generally used as the basis for any funboard competition, whether it's international, national, or just on a local level.

Course Racing
This is the first discipline in a funboard regatta, and is the most similar to the conventional form of triangle racing.

The standard course is shown here. You can see that it has a single very short beat, no runs, and a lot of reaching and gybing which puts the emphasis on funboard skills. In a WSMA regatta there is a requirement for a minimum Force 4 wind speed, but local funboard racing will usually opt for accepting less wind, and may use a simplified version of the course with less gybing.

Boards used for course racing are in essence the allround-funboards that you see in the shops. Typical length is about 3.60 m with anything from 180–210 litres volume, and the boards have daggerboards, mast tracks and footstraps so they can quickly change from beating to reaching trim. Depending on wind conditions, sails may be anything up to 7.5 sq m, with the better sailors opting for the biggest size possible to hit maximum speed on the reaches.

Many boards that were once

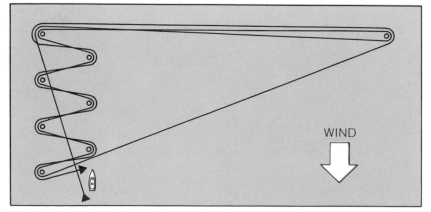

In World Cup course racing the boards start with a short beat to the first mark. They then have a long reach (minimum 800 metres) across the top of the course; gybe, and reach back along the same track; before a series of short reaches and quick gybes down to the Start/Finish line, where they commence the second round.

World Cup prototype course racers have gone into production after proving their worth – the F2 Lightning, Mistral Malibu, Fanatic Cat, Mistral Maui, Hi Fly Race, etc. The top World Cup sailors seldom race production boards, but use custom made prototypes that are lighter, stiffer, much more expensive, and just a little ahead of the designs that are already in the shops.

Slalom

Slalom evolved from the 'ins-and-outs' that were part of the famous Pan Am Cup in Hawaii. 'Ins-and-outs' means in and out through the surf – it calls for rough water and strong winds, which should not be confused with the light wind slalom that used to be a part of Windsurfer and other one-design regattas.

For funboard slalom the WSMA has a minimum wind speed require-ment of Force 5, which is a lot of wind. For club events the likely minimum is 11 knots, hopefully following the WSMA's re-commendation that 'slalom should be held through breaking surf'.

A typical slalom course starts from the beach with a sideshore wind. The sailors hold their boards and rigs ready for the off, and are usually limited to a maximum of eight competitors per heat with the

Midget Farrelly, Australian surfer turned windsurfer, performing in the Rip Curl Wave Classic. This is one of the major annual wave events, held each November at Point Danger near Torquay in Australia. In 'wave performance' the competitors sail man-on-man, doing freestyle on the waves in heats that get longer as they progress through to the finals.

top finishers going through to the next round on a knock-out basis.

The standard course is a figure-of-eight, with one mark close in by the shore. The sailors loop round four or five times before finishing back on the beach in a matter of minutes, completing a high speed race that relies on the best in funboard techniques.

Rules are kept simple, and are designed primarily for safety when boards may be travelling towards one another at well over 20 knots. Competitors going out through the waves have right of way over those coming in; and a competitor keeps clear while overtaking.

In 18 knot winds short custom boards of around 2.80 m are favoured, with rigs to suit the conditions. They must be very fast (hitting as much as 30 knots on the way back through the waves), but also be able to gybe cleanly at the marks and accelerate without stalling. In lighter winds, boards with more buoyancy of around 3.00 m will be preferred.

Wave Performance

After course racing and slalom, wave performance is the third WSMA discipline. It's really a freestyle competition on the waves, with sailors demonstrating their skills and being marked by a panel of judges in a similar manner to ice skating freestyle.

The first requirement is obviously waves, and the bigger they are the better. There should also be wind (minimum Force 4), which

will enable short custom boards to be used that are ultra manoeuvrable on a wave face.

The field is usually split into 'man-on-man' heats, with two competitors going on the water, vying against one another during the heat which is usually timed for around eight minutes. During that time each one will try to outdo the other for points, which are awarded for wave jumps, waveriding, and transitional gybes. A fluid performance is what generally gets the highest score, for there are no points in going for broke on one amazing ultra radical manoeuvre, and then spending the rest of the heat down in the water recovering. The competitors must also take care to stay within sight of the judges – there are no points if they are putting on a wonderful show when no one can see them!

Working through the heats in a wave performance event takes a lot of time and can seem complex. At the end of each heat the winner goes through his next heat on the 'winners' side', while the loser goes through to a heat on the 'losers' side'. This gives the loser a second chance, for the winner of the 'winners' side' eventually meets the winner of the 'losers' side' in the final of the competition.

Some rules are necessary in wave performance:

The competitor going out through the waves has right of way.
The first competitor to ride a wave has 'possession' and right of way while

both sailors are on it.
A competitor gybing, clear astern, or overtaking keeps clear.

Wave Performance Venues

The home of big waves and big wave events is Hawaii, and it's true to say that the sport of wave performance was invented there. Big dates in the annual calendar include the O'Neill Invitational and Maui Grand Prix held each spring and

Right: The most popular funboard slalom course is a figure-of-eight round two marks some 800 metres apart. Eight competitors start and finish on the beach, doing four or five circuits with the first four finishers going through to the next heat. The WSMA say 'the slalom course shall be set in surf where possible'.

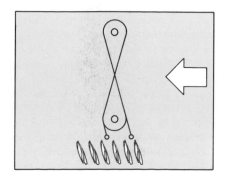

autumn at Hookipa; while Diamond Head usually hosts at least two events of equal importance.

Australia benefits from the same big waves as Hawaii, and the Rip Curl Wave Classic takes place each November at Point Danger in Victoria. Elsewhere in the world the waves are not so predictable, but World Cup and other funboard events include wave performance.

Amateur Funboard Racing

The WSMA also administer a World Amateur Funboard series, with national qualification regattas held throughout the season (approximately 200 events in 30 countries), with the finalists racing in the World Amateur Funboard Championship in the autumn. Only production boards (a minimum series of 500) can be used for course racing and slalom.

Above: Course racing in a British Fun Cup event at Llandudno on the north-west coast of Wales. The British Fun Cup is an annual series with regattas during the windier spring and autumn months. It includes course racing and slalom, but only allows production boards and rigs to be used and not prototypes. When conditions allow, wave performance is held on custom boards.

Wave Sailing

The Board

You can ride and jump waves with almost any board and rig – but with limited success. However in the past decade there have been many design and detail improvements to make things easier. Many boards are now sold as being suitable for sailing on waves, but as your ability develops so will the need for more specialized gear.

There are three basic categories of wave boards: the floater; semi-floater/marginal; and the sinker. As a sailor's ability advances he will progress through each of these.

Floaters are so named because they fully support the weight of the rig and rider. A floater over 3.20 m long can generally be tacked.

Marginals only partially support rig and rider when static. Pulling up the rig requires careful weight placement, and even so the board may be submerged during the procedure. Tacking will require lightning speed.

Sinkers do not support rig and rider in any substantial way, and therefore must be waterstarted. Volume is so low that there is no way they can be sailed if the wind drops; you should therefore be very sure of the weather and your level of experience before you attempt to sail one.

The volume of foam within a board determines how much weight it will support. Overall thickness and deck/rail profiles are other major factors, as well as length, width and to a lesser degree board weight. General extremes of wave sailing sizes are: length 2 m to 3 m; max width 50 cm to 65 cm; nose width (30 cm back from the nose) 28 cm to 43 cm; tail width (30 cm up from the tail) 28 cm to 48 cm.

Wide Versus Narrow Outline
Reducing width generally allows for more manoeuvrability. By re-taining or even adding width, over-all stability can be maintained. Generally, as a sailor improves, he will progress to narrower boards, and the loss in stability will go almost unnoticed.

The mean location of the widest point of the board is slightly forward of its middle. By moving it further forward the outline shape of the tail becomes straighter, and the effect is to improve board speed at the expense of manoeuvrability. Moving the wide point aft puts curve and hips into the outline shape of the tail. The planing area is increased allowing earlier planing, but maximum speed will be reduced by the resistance created by water being drawn into the more pronounced curve at the tail.

The wider the board the greater its planing surface, and in marginal conditions wide boards offer excellent performance. In higher winds their extra surface area will drag, and the tendency to bounce and skip will be much greater than with a narrower board, while responsiveness and turning ability will be lost.

Narrower tails extend the length of the planing surface, immersing more rail and thus increasing lateral resistance. The load on fins is thus reduced, while wide tails rely heavily on the fins to prevent sideslip, and are more prone to spin-out. The wider the tail, the more fins you need.

Scoop and Rocker
The standard formula for wave sailing is 2.5 cm of nose scoop for every 30 cm of length. Accentuating the curve in the last 15–30 cm helps 'pop' the nose out of the water should it ever bury. The curved nose flows into a relatively flat area around the mast foot from which speed is normally projected.

The last 45 cm of the board are critical to manoeuvrability. By adding tail rocker, turns are much more easily initiated. A standard amount of rocker on a 2.1–2.4 m board would be 3–4 cm measured from the fore and aft plane. Excessive tail rocker will slow the board.

Rail Profiles
The rails or outer extremities of the board accept and release water. Altering their shape vastly affects board handling and performance characteristics (see page 119).

Low hard rails (1) release water from the tail area with minimum influence on water flow from the bottom of the board. The clean release enhances speed, while in the nose this shape gives maximum lift.

Drawbacks are the likelihood of tripping the board on the rail at the nose as it digs into the water: and the tail bouncing and skipping since the clean release fails to press the board to the water.

A full, soft rail is the opposite extreme (2). The effect of this is to slow the board by keeping it hugging the water. The smooth flowing curve encourages water to flow up around the rail, submerging the board, and the large volume of foam in the rail aids flotation and stability. The drawback is that jumps are sluggish as the board fights to stay with the water.

Between these two extremes there are many compromises. The contemporary surfboard rail (3) is a good example, and a very popular choice. The maximum fullness of the rail is set at three-quarters depth, so that water tends to flow up around that first quarter to the fullest point, giving the board trac-

A typical wave board designed and made by the Naish Hawaii team of Rick Naish (Robbie's father) and Harold Iggy. Much of the design and development of this type of board stemmed from surfboard design where the same requirements of control and manoeuvrability hold true. Typical length is about 2.65 m, with the fairly wide tail designed for tight turns and good acceleration.

Waterstarts

Mastering the waterstart transforms strong wind sailing, and opens the door to shorter boards. It can be divided into three parts.

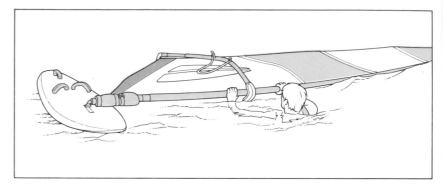

1 First you have to get the rig perpendicular to the wind, with the board pointing upwind. To do this it may be necessary to swim the rig round, and/or lift the clew to flip the sail. Then place your hands on the mast just by the boom.

2 Getting the rig up out of the water is the next task. To start with you will find it easiest to swim backwards at about 45 degrees into the wind, and at the same time lift the mast with your arms. Like a plane taking off this will get wind under the rig. As soon as the sail inflates pull the mast back down to just above the water until the boom end breaks free. Failure to do this will submarine the rig. With the boom clear you can get both hands in the sailing position. Continue kicking your legs which will keep the rig heading upwind, and push the board downwind onto a reaching position. You must trim the sail carefully according to the wind. Oversheeting will nosedive the board or tear the rig from your grasp.

3 The final stage is to get up. Place your back foot in the back strap when the board is in a beam reach position. Raise your arms, and bend your back leg to bring you in close to the board, which will expose maximum sail area.

4 Wait for sufficient pull in the sail, and then tread hard with your front leg and raise yourself up onto the board. You can then sail straight off on a reach.

Learning the waterstart is quite easy if you get rig and board in the right position; keep swimming the rig forward; get maximum lift from the sail.

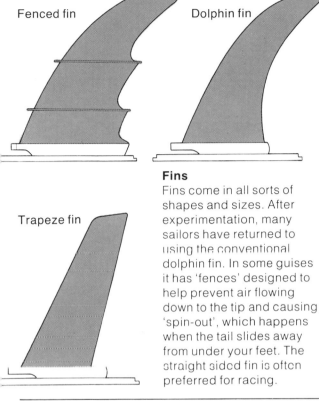

Fenced fin

Dolphin fin

Trapeze fin

Fins
Fins come in all sorts of shapes and sizes. After experimentation, many sailors have returned to using the conventional dolphin fin. In some guises it has 'fences' designed to help prevent air flowing down to the tip and causing 'spin-out', which happens when the tail slides away from under your feet. The straight sided fin is often preferred for racing.

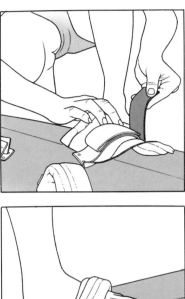

Footstraps
There are all kinds of different footstraps available. The most comfortable have overlapping layers of webbing held together with Velcro and covered by a soft outer sock. Note how far your foot goes in, with only the toes showing. If your foot could slip right through, there would be dangerous consequences after a bad fall with your ankle likely to be trapped in the strap.

---

tion without sluggishness. The tucked underedge permits a clean release, so the rider gains straight line speed, while the fullness of the rail helps prevent skipping and sliding when he carves turns.

Bottom Shape
The first 30 cm of the nose is best left flat, since if the nose touches this far forward the board is well on the way to purling (nose diving), and all available lift should be employed.

Behind this a completely flat nose entry area around the mast foot tends to slap and bounce, jarring ankles and knees. An elliptical curve (roll), rail to rail (5 mm–2 cm), gives the effect of standing on deep pile carpet rather than stone floor. A 'V' bottom shape has a similar beneficial effect, but the board will tend to bounce from one flat surface (chine) to the other.

The bottom area further aft is where the board's speed is derived

from, and the elliptical roll or 'V' tends to fade, though not completely, since at high speed this area will be the first point of contact with the water.

To gain manoeuvrability, a 'V' is used in the tail area which is most pronounced around the fins, and fades as the tail rocker increases. This allows the board to be rocked from rail to rail, as the curve of the planted rail describes the arc of the turn. A 1.25 cm maximum depth 'V' is enough to give really substantial benefits.

There is a great deal of opportunity for experimentation on bottom profiles. The 'V' and the curved bottom are thoroughly proven standards on which to base your experiments with drop wings, channels, double concaves, tunnels, triplanes, bevels etc.

Board Construction
The custom board is a very different story from something produced

by a major manufacturer in a matter of minutes (see Manufacturing Techniques). Employing the same materials and techniques as surfboard construction, the builder will spend many exacting hours on a single board.

There are several steps in custom board construction which a professional may specialize in. Shaping, airbrushing, and laminating are completed before fin boxes and textured deck are added. The board is then sanded and polished before the footstraps and mast foot are fitted.

Experience in shaping gives a sound insight into hydrodynamics – subtle changes in shape will affect performance remarkably. Lamination requires the handling of toxic chemicals and teaches the laminator correct balance of chemicals for the climatic conditions present.

To achieve maximum strength-to-weight ratio, the cloth should be barely saturated, and the resin

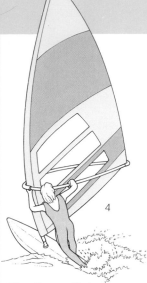

The Carve Gybe

Gybing for many is an awkward and tricky operation, and the difficulties are often related to the 'unnatural' body language required to execute the transition. However nothing looks more fluid than a planing carve gybe.

Wavesailing boards behave like skis. Turns are carved by weighting the inside rail. In order to practise carve gybes, a suitable board must be acquired. Try the following test to see how your board carves. Planing on a close reach with your feet in the straps, depress the toes and lift the heel of your front foot. *Excellent response* throws you and the board into a sweeping curve away from the wind, while *average response* means that the board will turn gradually away from the wind with no rig movements apart from sheeting in – the former is unlikely to happen on anything except a sinker with a narrow tail. *Poor response* is when the rail submerges to leeward with no direction change.

Initiating the gybe is a combination of techniques. Start the turn as for the test (**1**); thrust the hips to the inside of the turn and incline and twist the upper body as a cyclist would (**2**) with your back foot out of the strap and pushing down on the inside rail. Trim the rig

according to the wind direction and continue to concentrate on carving the board round. On the downwind course, board and wind speed should be closely matched with little power in the sail, so you rely on momentum to carry you through the turn. Let go with the sheet hand and grab the mast, letting the rig flip round onto the new side (**3**). Remember to keep carving the board, and grab the boom as soon as possible, before flattening the board out to sail off

on the new reach (**4**). You can then move your front foot out of the old front strap and into the new back strap, while sliding your other foot into the new front strap. Changing foot position after the gybe is particularly important, since it enables you to carve the board fluidly without upsetting its balance. You also need to be able to flip and sheet in the rig with minimum upset, and the technique requires a lot of practice before it is mastered.

should cure as soon as the lamination is complete to gain maximum strength. The work must be completed before the polyester resin cures.

Recent developments in lamination materials have produced superior cloths and resins.

A wavesailing board will be laminated with varying thicknesses. The bottom should have two layers of 6 oz which overlap the rail to give a strong four-layer lamination where it meets the two 6 oz layers on the deck. There should be a third overlay on the deck area from the mast foot to the tail of the board, and additional patches (four layers in all) in the footstrap positions; where the wishbone strikes the deck in the event of a wipe-out; and around the mast foot.

Polyester resin is most often used because of its easily controlled curing time. Standard blanks of polyurethane foam (Clark Foam) are suited to this resin, while slower-curing epoxy resin can also be used on polystyrene foam – the advantage of epoxy resin is that it is more flexible and thus less likely to shatter on impact.

If you wish to build your own board it will take several attempts before you get to a halfway decent standard. For the patient, diligent craftsman there is the chance to produce a board approaching professional standards within a year or two, but it is not easy, and you must seek professional advice.

Mast Location
Boards 2.75 or 3 metres long usually have the mast foot 1.8 m from the tail. 2.1 m and 2.5 m boards have them at 1.65 m and 1.8 m.

Footstraps
The straps should allow the feet to be slid in and out easily. A firm webbing makes the strap stand up rather than collapse on the deck.

Be sure the footstraps are spaced to allow a comfortable stance. Average stances vary from 50 to 60 cm.

Always position them for high wind sailing, since this is when they are really needed.

Textured Decks
Control of the board is greatly enhanced by a good firm grip. Nylon bag material is laminated on to the deck and after curing is ripped off. This provides an excellent deck texture.

Another method is to sift foam dust (excess from shaping) on to the resin. This gives a good grip but may require light sanding.

Finding the way back through a heavy shore break looks like a good time to damage a lot of equipment.

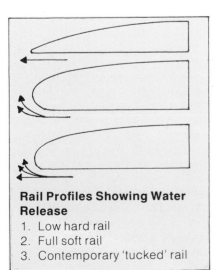

Rail Profiles Showing Water Release
1. Low hard rail
2. Full soft rail
3. Contemporary 'tucked' rail

The Rig

Mast, sail, booms and universal joint are subject to high stress in wave sailing. By reducing the over-all dimensions to a minimum, the rig can be made more manoeuvr-able, robust, and efficient, but few manufacturers produce equipment with the stresses of surf sailing in mind – you should be sure the gear you get has been tested in these conditions.

Sails

Wave sailors generally choose sails of 5.1 sq m and under. The reason is that any area greater than this offers relatively little more power, while severely limiting manoeuvra-bility and control. A high clew with the booms aligned at right angles to the mast is a virtual must for wave sailing, in order to keep the end of the wishbone clear of the water.

The Duck Gybe

A remarkable number of techniques have evolved for the performance of duck gybing, but this sequence shows the method most popularly used. The duck gybe is basically a carve gybe with a flamboyant extra thrown in which is not strictly necessary, but looks good on the water.

Start as for a conventional carve gybe, lifting on the front foot, and depressing the inner rail with your back foot out of the strap. The board needs plenty of momentum to get through the gybe. As you approach a downwind course, slide your back hand as far back along the boom as it will go (a short boom is obviously an advantage). Let go with your front hand, and pass it over your back hand to grasp the clew end of the boom (**1**). At the same instant let go with the old back hand (left hand in this sequence) so you can pull the boom over your head (**2**). With a normal high clew sail, a 'duck' isn't really needed. Grab the new boom as close to the mast as possible with your free hand (**3**). By this stage you should have carved the board right round to the new beam reach, and can grab hold of the boom with the other hand, sheet in, straighten out the board, and sail off.

The secret is to be able to gybe the sail effortlessly within a couple of seconds, while concentrating on carving the board through a full 180 degree turn without loss of speed.

When you're buying new, look for favourable points in the sail. It should have a long, low window filling most of the area beneath the booms so that you can see the waves, and make sure your path is clear of other windsurfers when you're gybing. It should also be very robustly constructed with plenty of reinforcement at the three corners. Handles for the outhaul and downhaul can be useful, and in particular a handle at the top of the sail can be invaluable for holding on to the rig when you're down in waves.

There are all sorts of hi-tech sail materials available, ranging from the conventional Dacron and Tery-lene style woven cloth to the plastic film laminates such as Mylar. When you're out in waves the advantages of light weight are much less important than durability, and the best advice is to opt for a sail made from a material which is well proven.

A good controllable sail maintains its centre of effort in a fairly constant position well forward in the sail. The way to test this is to sheet in normally and then gradually bring your hands close together. If control can be maintained when they are touching, then you have found an ideal sail, while a sail that leaves you struggling, pushing and pulling when your hands are shoulder width apart is thoroughly

The rider keeps the power on as he jumps from the face of the wave. You can see his track – the wave has already broken on either side.

unsuited to wave sailing.

In the early days of wavesailing the most popular rigs had pinhead and straight leech sails. Then battens started to appear to give more power at the top of the sail, and in particular the full length tapered battens which induce a stable curve into the front of the sail, which rotates so that it sets on the lee side of the mast. For wavesailing this is a mixed blessing. The power in a rotational sail tends to be fully on or fully off, and many of the top

Wave Jumping

There are many techniques of jumping employed in order to gain height, length, position in the air and control. Ultimately the techniques evolve into individual styles, but the basics follow the following formula.

Reaching at speed, feet firmly tucked into the straps, aim dead straight into the oncoming wave or 'whitewater'. The nose of the board is lifted as it rides up the ramp (**1**). Lean towards the tail – otherwise you may be pitched over the nose. If you intend to power the rig during flight (**2**) compensation must be made for the loss of lateral resistance from the fins and rail, for if the normal stance is maintained, the board will drift away downwind. The effect will be reduced if the sail is luffed during flight, but height, length and control are decreased.

To gain power and control through the jump, swing hips and upper body to leeward in over the board and towards the rig at the last moment before take-off.

Initially it may be difficult to convince your body to obey these instructions, but relax and the results will be promising. Keep sheeting in and leaning back. The board will respond to your foot and leg movements easily in the air. Press down on the toes of your back foot in order to lift the windward rail and expose the bottom of your board to the wind. The aerodynamic lift created by angling the board can significantly increase airtime.

During flight, endeavour to push the nose downwind by extending the front leg and powering the rig. The board will thus be pointing more directly on a downwind course when you land. Aim to land tail first (**3**), on the windward rail. Knees and ankles must flex a little to absorb the impact on landing.

Visualize the steps for a perfect jump in your mind before making the attempt. It is best to have worked them out ashore before you take to your board.

Hawaiian wavesailors turned back to sails with a single full length batten at the head, and short battens in the leech. There are always new ideas and designs to choose from. Some of these designs have been properly developed and tested, while others are mere gimmickry. If possible select proven designs from a reliable sailmaker, and try as many sails as possible in order to find out which ones suit you and the conditions best. Remember that as your abilities develop, so will your requirements in sails alter.

Masts

Of the scores of masts broken in the surf each year, most could be saved if the downed sailor guided his mast tip or wishbone end into the oncoming wave, holding it submerged as the wave struck. This is not always possible, and there are other reasons for breakages such as shore breaks and wipe outs.

Epoxy glassfibre masts are still preferred to alloy, with medium

flex characteristics being more resilient than stiffness. A soft mast won't give the sail sufficient support to hold its shape.

Once you have found a good mast, it is remarkable how long it stays in one piece, though reinforcement at the wishbone and base is a valuable precaution. The normal method is to use 4 in wide 6 oz glassfibre cloth soaked in resin.

Booms

The standard length wishbone for wave sailing is two metres maximum. For winds of 30 knots + you may use one as short as 1.3 m.

The reasons for this trend to shortness are many: trimming the sail becomes much less effort and thus the rig responds instantly; and the wishbone can be kept clear of the wave in tight situations, allowing the rider to manoeuvre closer to the critical section of the wave.

For a time wishbones were made very narrow in order to allow the sailor to get close to the rig. However with the development of sails

that have maximum fullness well forward, all that had to change. Booms are now usually wide at the mast end, becoming narrow at the outhaul end.

The boom ends should be compact, robust and functional. They should lock tight at the mast, preventing a loose and sloppy response due to rocking up and down. The clew end will strike the sea bottom frequently in shallow water wipe-outs, and a smooth profile will prevent it from catching on rock or coral. It is also less likely to cause any injuries to the sailor – from this point of view it is better to do away with cleats and tie the outhaul with half-hitches at the clew end of the wishbone.

It is important that the wishbone is exactly the right length for the sail, and if you have a quiver of three or more sails it is probably easiest to use a single adjustable wishbone which has a choice of end pieces to fit.

Below: With enough speed and a steep enough ramp, getting to this kind of height is surprisingly easy if you hit the wave square on by luffing up or bearing away as necessary.

Always aim to land on the tail, and try to eliminate spin-out by pulling in on your back leg and straightening the front so the tail is well upwind of the nose as you hit water. Don't land flat – it's bone jarring and can break the board. Don't land on the nose – it leads to accidents, and is best left to real experts.

Wave Sailing Technique

Outstanding performers have developed the ability to read waves from years of surfing experience. By predicting how a wave will break, a wave sailor is able to manoeuvre in the critical section of the wave – the part which is breaking and peeling – by using subtle body movements. Athletic prowess is desirable, but it plays a secondary role to knowing what's going on.

Waves break near the shore when the water depth is less than 1.3 times the wave height from trough to crest. Thus a 3 m wave will begin breaking in 4 m of water, but if the water then deepens, the crumbling lip will stop breaking

and re-form. If the depth decreases rapidly instead of crumbling, the crest will rise and pitch out a foaming 'tube', and then break with considerable violence.

The Beach
It may not be your burning desire to prove your brilliance to an audience on shore, but falling around amongst fragments of broken mast in the shorebreak rarely gives joy to the unfortunate sailor.

The first priority is a feasible launching site. If rideable waves are breaking outside, then the shoreline is unlikely to be calm. A plunging overhead shorebreak is difficult, and gets impossible in stronger winds.

Look for a gentle slope on the shore. This is likely to be best protected. Watch and get a feel for the rhythm of the shorebreak and

judge approaching waves. When you're confident you've found the right place, carry the board down to the water.

Grab the mast with your windward hand just below the wishbone, and the front windward footstrap with your other hand. Raise the nose of the board by pulling up with the mast hand, while keeping the board level with the back hand. If your board is nose heavy and awkward to transport like this, simply cant the mast across in front of your forehead, and support the rig and nose of the board with your head pushing up on the sail window.

Getting Out
The most suitable wind direction for wave sailing is *sideshore*, with a tolerance of 45 degrees either side. It's best of all if the wind is blowing

Waveriding relies much more on technique and expertise than strength.

When the wind veers *offshore*, it is liable to be gusty. Returning to the shore will require sailing partially upwind with the waves being used to assist progress. Sailing out through whitewater is made easy, since the waves can be approached directly with optimum speed on a broad reach, though the lee side of the wave is liable to harbour turbulent conditions. Obviously an offshore wind will to some extent flatten the waves.

If you sail out on a close reach in offshore winds, remember to lift the leeward rail (which will hit the wave first) to direct the board up and over, rather than into the wave. The board will tend to be thrust shoreward and into the wind, and therefore the power on the rig is liable to increase dramatically, launching an unprepared rider into his sail. To counter this, depress the windward rail and lean back against the rig as the whitewater pushes the board shorewards.

In the Waves
Having dealt with the small mushy waves of a shorebreak (in tidal areas they are at their smallest at low tide), you may need to face sets of bigger waves further out. These may be rising up and breaking on an area of shallow ground such as a reef (a 'reef break') or sand bar, and if you know what you're doing this makes an excellent area for wavesailing. If you don't you are likely to get severely munched.

Hitting an oncoming wall of whitewater tilts the sailor forward. To counter this and help lift the nose, transfer your weight to the back foot and use your knees to absorb the rise in the board. The board will be slowed, but pumping the rig will bring it back to a plane much more swiftly.

Approaching the last breaking wave requires anticipation of its peeling action. The whitewater is most turbulent as the wave initially breaks, while beside it the un-broken wave offers the highest and steepest sections to jump. At first it is wise to stay away from this critical section, since a few tenths of a second will make all the difference between a tail-first and a nose-first landing – the latter is highly undesirable and will be induced by the wave breaking over the nose as you begin to take off. At this point, baling out and throwing the rig and board clean away is the safest course of action.

Riding or surfing waves back towards the shore in more onshore winds causes a substantial reduction in the apparent wind, as the board and the wind begin travelling in much the same direction. Thus the board is heavily relied on for directional control, and since little drive is coming from the rig, it will tend to feel mushy and unresponsive.

Marginal Conditions
Riding a short board, the sailor is dealing with a twitchy, sensitive tool. Weight placement becomes critical. To gain good speed in marginal planing conditions, pumping helps but is wasted unless board trim is good. Keeping the board level from rail to rail, with weight forward so as to bring the nose about 15 cm clear of the surface, helps speed greatly. If the board is showing a tendency to drop off the plane, lean all your weight forward onto the mast foot to prevent the tail sinking and hopefully get it planing again.

Getting *upwind* without a daggerboard is achieved in one of two ways. In heavy airs, getting on the plane and just carrying it as close to the wind as possible works well, but in lighter winds when planing is hard to sustain on a close reach, a second technique is required. Push the windward rail deep in the water and by moving forward extend the waterline length of the board to its maximum – the board then behaves like a long daggerboard.

parallel to the shore, since waves can be caught both left and right, and you get a good speed going out through the whitewater.

When the wind blows *onshore*, cutting through whitewater at speed is less easy. On a beam reach the waves will strike the windward rail of the board from nose to tail, and heading up into the oncoming whitewater and lifting the windward rail will help guide the board cleanly up and over. Otherwise the board is liable to be washed shoreward and to leeward, causing the rig to lose power and come down on top of the sailor. This is where waterstarts come in useful – just wait for the whitewater to pass over your head.

Speed Sailing

Dutch born Jaap van der Rest has made a speciality of speed sailing, and in particular the World Speed Sailing Record.

In 1980 he broke this 500 metre record when he sailed a Windsurfer Special at an average of 24.45 knots. He then went on to push the record to 25.1 knots in 1981, before this record was obliterated by the Frenchman Pascal Maka at Weymouth in 1982, whose 27.82 knot run broke the 50 kph barrier.

Jaap started windsurfing when he was fourteen, and raced for three or four years until he got fed up with the rules and the ultra-serious attitude of the competitors. He then joined the Ten Cate team with their special speed boards designed by Californian Gary Seaman, sailing with them for two years until he first broke the record.

What does it take to sail through a course that fast? As a discipline it bears very little relation to triangle racing, wave riding, freestyle, or any of the other aspects of specialized windsurfing.

It revolves solely around the sailor who can propel his windsurfer fastest through a 500 metre course with his run officially timed. There are major 'speed trials' in the UK (Portland Harbour near Weymouth is the original), France, Germany, Holland and Hawaii, where precise timing is available. The boards that attend them are specially built for the purpose.

Most speed trials are set up so that the boards can reach through the course, sailing as broad a reach as possible. Ideal conditions are a flat sea with a lot of wind, and half the competitor's skill lies in keeping going until he gets the right run.

During 1981 Jaap took part in the three major World Speed Trials; and broke his own record. By following his explanation of what took place at them one can get some idea about what happened in the world of speed boards, where there was a single very radical development. The three speed trials took place in Weymouth, Brest and Veere, and each one has its own very different character. More recently Port St Louis in France has superseded Brest and Veere.

Weymouth
The speed trials in Weymouth are the oldest ones of all, and their character is typically English.

Until a few years ago only enthusiastic eccentrics took part,

Left: Van der Rest at speed on the board he used in Weymouth and Brest, before he became convinced that Jürgen Honsheid had found the answer to going faster by sailing a simple surfboard.

arriving at the start in outrageous looking vessels – the event is open to any sailing craft, and not only windsurfers.

Many of these odd craft never really worked. Their masts bent, the hull (or hulls) broke in half, and sometimes the owner would spend the whole week tinkering on the beach without putting to sea at all.

In 1981 the situation at the Weymouth trials had changed from previous years. Windsurfers had

totally taken over the 10 Square Metre category, squeezing out all the other sailing craft, and the World Record holder *Crossbow* decided not to participate. She had recorded 36 knots, and with 180 square metres of sail did not want to take the risk of colliding with one of the smaller craft.

There were a variety of interesting boards present. A stepped board with a pintail stern seemed a good idea, since it would plane on

Above: In April 1985 Austrian Michael Pucher pushed the World Speed record to 32.35 knots at Port St Louis near Marseilles.

the front of the step and the last 40 centimetres of the board alone; there was the Carlsberg Special, but that never seemed to go afloat; there was the previous record holder Clive Colenso, experimenting with an aluminium honeycomb construction; and last but not least

127

there were the Gary Seaman designed Ten Cate boards for Erika and Jaap Keller, Jan Marc Schreur, and myself.

Things started well when I put in the fastest speed on the first day of 22.9 knots. I expected to win the week with ease.

A few days passed quietly, and then I had a rude awakening. The West German/Hawaiian maestro Jürgen Honsheid had turned up with a stock Tiki surfboard, the only board to have less volume and wetted surface area than my own. He stuck a windsurfer rig up near the bow, and then proceeded to sail up and down the course as if he was out in Force 4 – in fact it was blowing near Force 9!

I broke my skeg, another sailor broke his ribs, and Jürgen broke my record with a run of 24.75 knots – but it wasn't fast enough to beat my record by the required 2 per cent (to allow for timekeeping inaccuracy) so I was allowed to keep it!

Brest

Four days were left to prepare for the Speed Cup in Brest on the north-west corner of France. I was worried about Jürgen, but I expected to beat him when I had repaired my skeg.

The Brest week is set up very differently from Weymouth. Four sponsors were present in great style, with prizes, press, entertainment every night, and a gigantic wall of televisions to tell the spectators what was happening.

They laid a big circular course just like the one on Portland Harbour, but the trouble was that it was at least four kilometres offshore, and it therefore suffered from many disadvantages.

The spectators were stuck with televisions rather than seeing the real thing; it took a long time to sail out to the course; the waves were enormous whenever the wind started to blow; and there was absolutely no control of the starting

Above: Hawaiian Fred Haywood became the first man to break 30 knots when he pushed the record to 30.82 knots at Portland in 1983. He used a special wing rig.

Below: The 'conventional' Weymouth speedcraft have been gradually pushed out by the windsurfers, even though their entries have been limited.

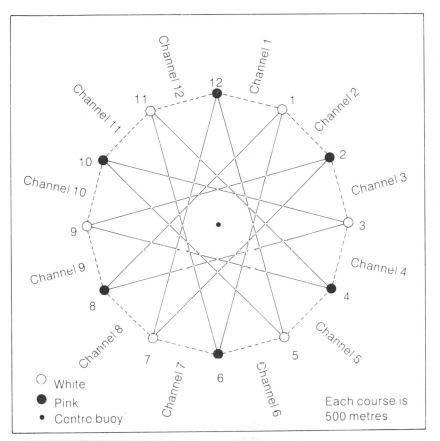

Channel 1
Channel 2
Channel 3
Channel 4
Channel 5
Channel 6
Channel 7
Channel 8
Channel 9
Channel 10
Channel 11
Channel 12

○ White
● Pink
• Centre buoy

Each course is 500 metres

Left: The Portland Harbour course is laid out by the RYA each October hopefully to coincide with the equinoctial gales. They lay a circle of buoys, with one buoy in the centre, so that entrants have a choice of 12 Channels with a direct distance of 500 metres – they choose the Channel that best suits their angle of attack.

When it blows very hard, this course becomes too rough for the windsurfers to sail fast through the waves, and the RYA lays on an alternative single Channel 'inshore course' which runs parallel to the beach in shallow water. This is where the boards achieve their best speeds, though they are frequently limited by the angle of the wind to the course.

Below: Jurgen Honsheid at Weymouth in 1981, and about to give Jaap van der Rest a very nasty shock. His board is so small you can barely see it amid the spray. Jürgen learnt his techniques for this type of sailing in Hawaii.

procedure. As a result, whenever there was a good gust, the course changed into a kind of Champs Elysees during the rush hour.

The last straw was the large number of offshore trimarans and catamarans which the organizers had encouraged to take part in the event. I was run down by one, and then they deliberately sabotaged the inshore course which was used on the one day when it blew hard. They sailed across it, and then lay idle in the middle of it. It goes without saying that these incidents did not improve the atmosphere.

However the presence of the RYA observer, Sir Reginald Bennett, did benefit the atmosphere. Sir Reginald is very aristocratic, and very popular with the sailors. His speeches are unusual in being excellent, and he was the only person to attack the French publicly for giving such precedence to these large boats.

Erika Keller found time to become 'la plus vite femme du monde' with a speed of 20.3 knots. She won 12,500 francs for her trouble, while I found that Jürgen was still going faster than me – the smaller wetted surface area of his board was proving decisive.

Veere

I had two weeks to design and build a new board for the Pall Mall Speed Trials in Veere.

First I modified an ordinary surfboard into a windsurfer and started to practice on it. With the information from this I then built a new board in the remaining four days.

The finish of the board left much to be desired, and then there was no wind for my planned test days. So, there I was at the Veere Speed Trials with a board I had never sailed before, and which might need a lot of alterations. Yet I had no other choice, for I knew that Honsheid would beat me if I sailed my old board.

The Pall Mall Speed Trials are unique. The timing is by video cameras and is accurate within hundredths of a second; the course is so near to the shore that the public can easily follow the event; and the safety boat back-up for competitors is excellent.

The week started with very light winds. On the third day I put in quite a fast time – and then on my last run on Friday 13th November I broke the record with a new speed of 25.2 knots.

Coming Up To Date

By the speed trials of autumn 1982, every competitor was relying on a sinker and a great deal of wind. At Brest, Philip Pudenz set a new record of 26.5 knots, but it was short lived, for Pascal Maka ran at 27.82 knots at Weymouth two weeks later. Six other sailors exceeded 26 knots, all using very similar short boards, while Jaap van der Rest could only manage 25.2 knots.

The next breakthrough came in 1983 when Fred Haywood came to Weymouth and increased the record to 30.82 knots. Fred used a tiny Sailboards Maui board (designed by Jimmy Lewis) with a big Neil Pryde rig that featured a carbon fibre wing mast. This precipitated all sorts of hi-tech rigs during 1984, but most of them proved too difficult to use and the record remained unbroken.

In the spring of 1985 speed trials were held at a new venue at Port St Louis on the French Mediterranean coast near Marseilles. This benefitted from a Force 9 Mistral wind blasting down from the Rhone Valley, and the result was that 12 sailors broke Haywood's record with Michael Pucher taking the fastest time at 32.35 knots.

Other Records

Most speed trials attract at least half a dozen tandems, the most extreme of which are no more than two-man

sinkers. During 1985 the tandem record stood at 27.43 knots.

The ladies also have a speed record which was first set by Jenna de Rosnay in 1982. She lost it to Marie Annick Maus in 1983, winning it back at Weymouth the following year with a run of 27.2 knots.

The outright speed record is still held by the 60 foot proa Crossbow at 36 knots.

Speed Boards

After the sinker was accepted as the fastest type of speed board, designs have settled down with all the top competitors sailing similar size and shape boards. Simplicity, ease of sailing, and the skill of the sailor are the most important considerations when trying to achieve an average speed of over 32 knots.

Rigs are also kept simple, and are virtually 'off the shelf' products with a favoured size around 5.0 sq m for 30 knots of wind.

The typical speed board is around 2.50 m long with a long thin gun profile, no more than 25 cm wide. Bottom shape is likely to feature very slight double concaves and V with a single fin, with ultra stiff and ultra light construction using exotic materials such as epoxy and carbon kevlar over a polystyrene core.

Trying for the tandem record. This is Peter Hart and Dee Caldwell at Weymouth in 1984, sailing the Carlsberg Special. Campaigning a board like this can be expensive, and sponsorship is welcome.

Many of these boards are home built by enthusiast speed sailors. Materials are inexpensive, and so long as the board works, finish is unimportant.

Freestyle

Freestyle windsurfing developed from an elaborate excuse to fall into the water to a combination of gymnastics and ballet. It includes pirouettes and flips, jumps and splits. There are competitions world wide with freestylists entered. We have judges, rules, compulsory tricks, and fixed routines. It's even grown to the point that there are freestyle specialists – sailors who do only freestyle. None of this complexity, however, can diminish the primary appeal of freestyle – it's still a heck of a good excuse to fall into the water.

1976 was the year Ken Winner's interest in freestyle surfaced. He was twenty one and had little better to do than spend hours away from school splashing about in the water attempting Head Dips and Water Starts. English literature and calculus had little chance against the water's lure on a warm, breezy spring day. It's ironic that his hours on the water have given him a better vocation than time in the classroom ever could.

'76 was also the year of the Railride. Railriding had been done before, but Robby Naish, then only 12 years old, brought a better technique to North America and then the world. The Railride became the most appealing trick around that year, the fanciest thing you could do on a board, and it focused considerable attention on freestyle windsurfing. Doing freestyle, riding the rail, was how you showed the crowd at the beach that you weren't just another boardsailor. Boys became men through the simple act of putting a sailboard on edge.

The following year freestyle became an event at the Windsurfer World Championships in Sardinia, Italy. With this new distinction came controversy. Who should the judges be? Should there be a large penalty for falls? Should spectacular tricks or graceful tricks be encouraged? Never mind what the

Above: American born Ken Winner, one of the early World Freestyle Champions, a winner of the Pan Am Cup, runner up in the first two World Cup series, and funboard designer for Bic.

judges say, who really won? Each year at major freestyle competitions these questions are asked, and answered. The answers change as the sport evolves, as the competitors become more skilled and the judges more perceptive, but the questions remain the same. It is the presence of these questions, these controversies, that show freestyle's vitality, its appeal to a broad range of people.

That range of people includes the competitors, of course, but more importantly, it includes the many sailors who do freestyle for neither glory, nor money, but rather for fun: the fun of being in the open air, feeling the wind in

hand and the water under foot, the pleasure of seeing the world upside-down through a Head Dip, or the giddy sensation of twirling in a Pirouette.

It also includes people who enjoy the challenge of a new trick, the satisfaction of learning it well, and who in turn want to teach it to a friend. And it includes those who just need a good excuse to fall into the water.

Right: British Freestyle Champion Dee Caldwell demonstrates the *Everole* as part of his routine. Dee mastered the art of freestyle by training in the Bahamas during the winter months.

Somersaulting through the wishbone looks good if you can manage to fit between the wishbone and the sail, and land back on the board while keeping sailing. However it's difficult, and most sailors use it as the 'dismount' part of their routine, when they are happy to finish up in the water with a big splash.

The Background

Freestyle has developed from 'hot dogging' which was an undisciplined way of having fun on a board.

The Americans were first to develop it into a proper routine, and it was the American born Windsurfer class that began to run competitions similar to the freestyle events familiar to skaters.

That was the 1970s, and since that time routines have got slicker, and more and more polished. The time when a railride was greeted by exclamations is long gone, and now it's the people who can't do it who stand out like a sore thumb – and freestyle competitions are held during many weekend regattas.

Freestyle and Its Uses

There are not many top regatta sailors who can't at least manage the basics of freestyle. The ability to know the limits of a board's manoeuvrability are vital when you're juggling for position on a windy start line, or rounding a mark with a mass of other boards when there will inevitably be collisions.

For instance, at the start you frequently need to sail backwards away from the line; if you fall off, it's a lot quicker to be able to recover with a water start; and when you infringe the rules, it's time for a high speed 720 degree turn, which only a freestylist knows how to do best – by mastering a freestyle routine, you can get out of all these unexpected messes.

Freestyle Routine

The normal pattern in a regatta is for each contestant to be allotted three minutes in which to perform his or her routine. The signal for starting is when the contestant drops one arm, and then the judges loud-hail him when the time is up, with a 30 second warning and a 15 second countdown.

Freestyle Judging

The contestant needs to perform a wide variety of tricks with a smooth and stylish transition from one to the next.

In a big international competition, there will be four judges who will evaluate the performance in each of the following categories:
1. Number of tricks performed.
2. Technical difficulty of tricks performed.
3. The originality of the routine.
4. Style in the execution of the tricks.
5. Style in the execution of the routine as a whole.

Each category is marked out of 20, and the marks of the four judges are averaged out. When there are a great many competitors,

there will be preliminary rounds, quarter and semi finals, and finals.

In smaller local events it is only necessary to have two or three judges, and you can work out a simpler marking system – competitors don't often argue with the judges. If the standard is low, you can make do with shorter routines of two minutes or less.

It's not in the normal tricks repertory, but there are occasional competitions for two-up freestyle, and if you can juggle, why not? The normal combination for this kind of thing is a father and his very small son, or a boy and his girlfriend, but it's seldom taken very seriously. However, it can bring some light relief to a regatta.

Preparation and Basics

The ideal freestyle board should be a flatboard with wide deep rails, which is stable and easy to sail, but at the same time responsive and quick to manoeuvre.

Typical favourites are the Windsurfer Regatta and Mistral Competition. They frequently have a cutdown skeg to help the board turn really fast – sailing in a straight line is not a requisite of a good freestyle routine!

Vital Points

A freestyle board needs as careful preparation as a board for regatta racing or wave jumping.

Non-slip. There is no way you should slip on that board. If there is any chance of doing so, use board wax, and not just on the deck. When you're railriding you'll need to use the sides and bottom, so wax those as well.

Mast foot. Under no circumstances should it come out, and you will be putting constant pressure on it to see you and your board through a trick – you spend a lot of time levering the mast against the deck of the board in order to keep it up on the rail. Screw it up really tight, or if that won't work, tape it up and hammer it in.

Daggerboard. When you're on the rail you'll want to step on and off it, so wax it as well. Make sure it's not a sloppy fit which will slide out when you flip up the board. On the other hand you don't want it jammed in rock solid – it's handy to pull it halfway so that you can use it as a step on the deck side of the board when you're going on to the rail.

Sails

You should also consider which sail to use. When you're developing and learning tricks it's best to have a light wind, but when you do your award winning routine you need plenty of power in the sail to support those body dips and somer-saults. If the sail is too small or too flat you'll be dropping into the water in the middle of every trick, so make sure it's easily handled and the right size – the ideal is a high clew short boom sail with a steady Force 3 wind over a pancake flat sea.

Clothing

The fewer clothes you wear, the more agile you are – but that's only OK if the water is warm and you're experienced enough not to get covered in bruises and bashes.

When you start, you'll find that your shins and feet are particularly susceptible – you'd do best to wear a long john with reinforced shin pads, and some windsurfing shoes that grip like limpets.

Basic Tricks

All freestylists should learn to master the basic tricks before they move on to the more rarefied variations and their own inventions – there's always someone who comes up with something new and startling just once or twice a year!

These are the basic tricks which were worked out by the Windsurfer class all those years ago:

Quick tack
Like it says.

Quick Gybe
Likewise.

Power Gybe
Pushing the board through the eye of the wind by forcing the rig against the wind to turn the board. Much used in racing and strong wind sailing.

Head Dip
Sticking your head in the water while sailing – you can do it either backwards or forwards. It's good exercise for your back.

Body Dip
Lowering your body in the water while still sailing – and then letting the rig lift you out again.

Water Start
Not that dissimilar to the above. Starting sailing when you're lying in the water is useful when you have an inadvertent fall during your freestyle routine. Also much used by those sailing short funboards.

Stern First
Sailing along with your stern leading the way.

Inside the Wishbone
Sailing along with your body stuck up between the wishbone and the sail. You can do it on the windward or the leeward side.

Leeward Side Sailing
Standing there, pushing the rig from the leeward side while you're sailing along.

Back to the Sail
Doing the above with your back to the sail, and looking very cool.

Sitting
Like it says.

Lying
Ditto, and you can go so far as to try the splits.

Sail 360
Turning the rig through 360 degrees while the board keeps sailing in a straight line. Alternatively you can try a board 360 which will come in useful when you have to do all those penalty 720s on the race course.

Railride
Flip the board up on its side and stand on the rail. There are many variations: you can go backwards; forwards; inside the wishbone; etc.

Tail Sink
Sinking the back end, which is useful for nice slow gybes.

Dismount
Any way you want to finish your routine, so long as it is dramatic/graceful. Climb to the top of the mast, somersault through the wishbone, or simply catapult into mid air. It's important to get the timing right, and if it's good you'll raise a cheer from the spectators.

Flying high with a tail-sink as the culmination of a freestyle routine. Finishing off with a dramatic trick is all part of impressing the judges.

Basic Railride
Sail along on a reach. To flip the board up, push down on the leeward rail with your back foot, while pulling up the windward rail with your front foot. At the same time take some of your weight on the wishbone, and the board will flip up easily. Rest your shin on the rail, or put your forward foot on the daggerboard for comfort. Then try putting both feet on the rail, and sail in a squatting position. You can then stand up, pushing with your feet and pulling with the rig to keep the board on the rail.

First Attempts
You should learn trick by trick. Pick out the one you want to do, and then work at it until you've got it right, rather than giving up and going on to the next one.

If you can, rehearse the trick on dry land. You'll find that you can run through almost the whole routine, including railrides.

When you come to try the trick on the water, make sure it's flat, shallow, with the wind around Force 2. Ideally the water should be warm as well.

Working out a Routine
Master your individual tricks until you've got each one right – in light winds, medium winds, and strong winds.

You can then string them together into a routine, where one trick should lead on gracefully to the next.

There is no way you can do this by intuition alone. Sure, you have to know enough to improvise and grab opportunities if something goes wrong or conditions change, but your basic routine for those three minutes should have been worked out to perfection by you months before.

Favourites
All the tricks are variations on a theme of good board control. These are favourites for a good freestyle routine.

Railride
This is the one you have to be able to do. When you get really good, you can do it backwards, forwards, inside the wishbone, to windward or to leeward of the rig, and on (what was) the windward or leeward rail of the board. You can also rock 'n' roll it as you go along.

The basic railride is a matter of balance, and preventing the board from heading up into the wind, which it will always be inclined to do. You should be sure to master the simple art of flipping up the windward rail and sailing along, before you move on to any of the more ornate variations on this theme. If you find you're slipping on the board, you can rough up the surface with a rasp.

Right: The fine art of balancing on the rail is the basis of a freestyle routine. Once you have mastered it you can improvise a succession of different tricks, illustrated on the following pages.

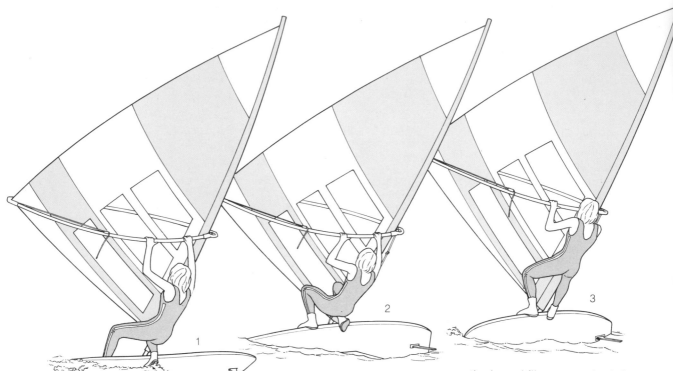

Railride Backwards
Sail the board backwards, travelling skeg first. Push down on the lee rail with your back foot while lifting the windward rail with your front foot (**1**). At the same time take your weight on the wishbone, and as the board flips up put both feet on the rail (**2**) and stand up (**3**). A relatively flat board such as the Windsurfer will sail as well backwards as forwards when it's up on the rail like this. More variations follow.

Railride Variations

A world class freestyle sailor can sail on the rail rather better than most of us can sail with the board flat on the water, but it just takes hours of practice.

Railriding heading backwards is a little more difficult than the basic technique, and railriding on the leeward rail is a little more difficult still.

An interesting variation on the lee side railride is the 'Everoll' developed by American Gary Eversole, who also invented the 'Rock 'n' Roll' (on boards). The Everoll is a railride taken just a little too far. You sail clew first to the wind, and then flip up the leeward side of the board, letting it rest against the mast when it comes up, so that you can stand on the daggerboard on the bottom of the windsurfer. Once you're set up like this you can control the angle of the board by sheeting in and out. Obviously it is important that the daggerboard is fixed fairly firmly in place.

Recovery

If you mess it up and fall in, it is imperative that you can recover as neatly and swiftly as possible. A water start is the smartest way to start up again.

The easiest way to learn the basics of a water start is to let yourself fall back into the water on purpose. Sail along on a reach, and then let out your sheet hand so that you fall back with the rig on top of you.

So long as you lift the rig clear of the water, and keep the board beam on to the wind, you will find that once you sheet back in, the rig will lift you out and back on your feet.

If the wind is light it's tricky, and you may need to give it a helping hand. Bend your knees to

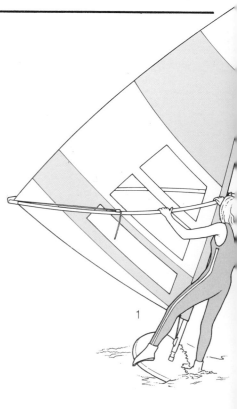

get your weight inboard, and if that's no good shift your hands down from the wishbone to the base of the rig. The mast hand can hold the rig a couple of feet above the deck, while the sheet hand grabs the foot of the sail about one-third of the way back. This way the rig should have enough leverage to lift you right out again. Remember that the board will want to head up into the wind. Obviously it's easier if you're a lightweight.

Right: Dee Caldwell sitting on the rail and looking very wet. His next move will be to tuck his feet up so he can stand on the rail.

Reverse Railride

Sail along on a reach and start to push down the windward rail (**1**). At the same time help to lift the leeward rail with your other foot, while taking your weight on the wishbone (**2**). As the board flips up, stand on the rail (**3**). You can then move one foot forward of the mast for your next trick (**4**).

This is a lot trickier than a conventional railride, since you need a lot more balance to keep the board up on the rail. You must play the pressure of the mast against the side of the board very carefully, or it will flip back down again. This is when it is particularly important to have the mast foot jammed solidly into position – there must be no way that it can come unstuck during your routine.

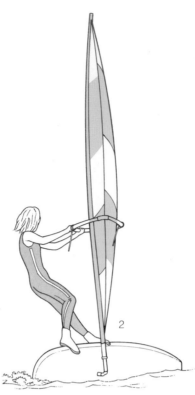

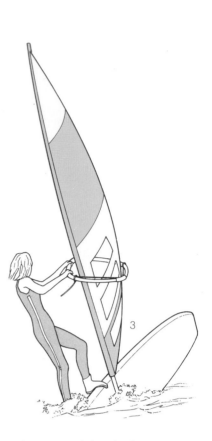

Rock 'n' Roll

Sail along on the rail, either forwards or backwards. With your feet spread fairly well apart, you can then rock the board, dipping the nose and the stern alternately. It is important not to slip, and to try and do this trick gracefully with an easy motion. A lot of sailors do it very jerkily and in a hurry, and it just looks a mess.

This trick was first seen at the Windsurfer World Championship in Sardinia in 1977, and has been part of the repertoire ever since.

Waterstart Practice

You can practise the basics of the waterstart on the beach and in shallow water. As well as being important for this kind of freestyle, it's a vital technique for funboard sailing.

The main point to remember in freestyle is that you don't have time to go through the whole waterstart procedure (explained in detail on page 116). When you drop in you must keep the rig above the surface of the water, on the windward side of the board which can be facing forwards or backwards, depending on which direction you want to sail off in. If necessary, you must be able to waterstart clew-first.

Left: Power and precision as a sailor pirouettes during his freestyle routine. Tricks should always be graceful. To win you should be as impressive and as fluid as an ice skating champion.

Body Drag

If it's windy enough, and the board is travelling fast, you can come near to walking on water.

Sail along on a broad reach, and then simply step backwards off the board on to the water. You won't be able to run fast enough to keep up with it, but you can allow your body to be towed like an old bundle for a few seconds. When the rig starts collapsing or the board starts bearing off, it's time to pull in with your arms and get back on the board pretty smartly.

This trick would look good as a lead-up to a somersault through the wishbone, followed by a flare gybe to get you going back in the opposite direction.

Finally, whatever you do, don't get carried away during your routine with a sequence of tricks on one tack that ends up two miles from the judges! They don't appreciate having to use binoculars!

Back to the Boom

A good basic trick to get the hang of is sailing with your back to the leeward side of the sail. It looks easy and it looks cool.

You start off by building up speed on a close reach. Then, let your sheet hand go and grab the mast a couple of feet down from the wishbone. At the same time let go with your mast hand, and step round the front of the mast so that you're on the lee side of the sail.

Railride Inside the Wishbone

This is a lot more difficult than it looks, and needs a lot of practice if you're not going to end up falling in. It's also a difficult trick to recover from gracefully if you do fall in, so don't put it in your routine until you know you're not going to mess it up.

Sail along on a regular railride – it doesn't matter whether it's nose or stern first. Be sure to keep a fairly broad reach, and when you're comfortable (**1**), tuck your head up inside the wishbone, supporting it with the back of your neck (**2**). You can then wriggle your body through, while keeping a firm grip on the wishbone with your hands and arms (**3**). Once you're up

inside the wishbone, you have to be very careful not to let the board round up head to wind. Remember that your movement is limited, so it's difficult to respond quickly to any gusts. It's best if you move

your forward hand to the mast (**4**), which will at least give you a little more leverage and response from the rig. This should always be raked well forward.

A trick like this should flow on as a continuous part of a railride, and can be combined with other specialities such as rock 'n' roll and gybing on the rail, before reverting to some tricks, such as helicopters and hirondelles, which are accomplished when the board is flat on the water. If you want to do these tricks in the right sequence, you must learn from watching the top sailors.

Railride Clew-first

You can sail with the rig turned 180 degrees the wrong way, so that the clew is pointing into the wind. It's not as efficient as sailing with the rig the right way round, but it does work.

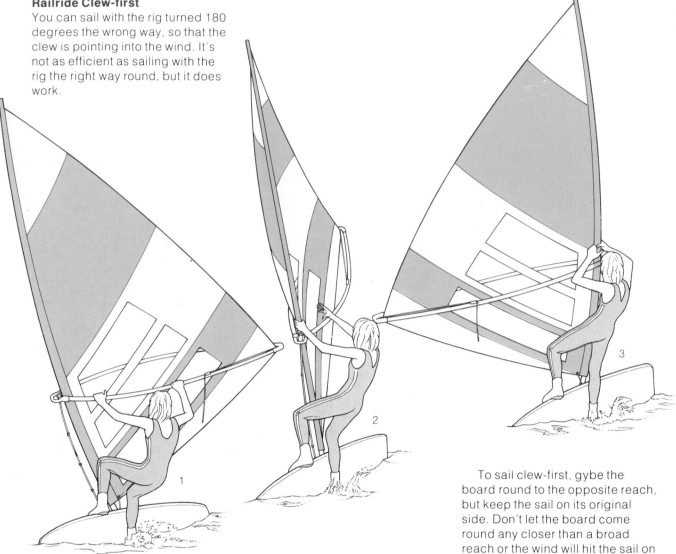

To sail clew-first, gybe the board round to the opposite reach, but keep the sail on its original side. Don't let the board come round any closer than a broad reach or the wind will hit the sail on

You can then change the hand holding the mast, and rake the rig forward as you push back with the other arm outstretched along the wishbone to sheet in and get sailing.

You must remember to keep on a reach. Don't let the board head up or bear away too much, or it will deposit you in the water.

Spin Tack

There's nothing too difficult about this, and it looks pretty good.

Go into a regular tack, but when you step round the front of the mast give a little 180 degree spin on the ball of your foot so that you end up turning through a full 360 degrees.

As you turn, you can grab the rig as necessary if you feel it's going AWOL. So long as your timing is alright, everything will be OK.

Wheelie

A Tail Sink looks pretty clumsy in light winds. The guy just sinks the back of the board, and then clambers back along it to flatten it out.

However if it's windy you can turn it into a full wheelie.

Sail along on a very broad reach

as fast as you can – and then jump on to the very back of the board with all your weight. It's the same process as slowing down for the gybe mark, but hopefully the board will delight the judges as it skips along on its stern before it finally goes down into a regular tail sink.

At this point you can always go into a flare gybe, and head back on the other reach as you prepare for your somersault-on-the-rail routine, which would be a nice way to finish your three minutes. Anyone who invents a new trick is going to score heavily.

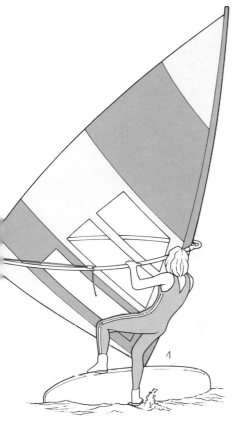

its lee side and take control of you. You can flip the board up on the rail in the conventional manner (**1**), though you will need to keep one foot on the daggerboard to prevent the board flipping right over. You can then gybe the rig (**2/3**) and sail on in the conventional railride position (**4**). Going from tack to tack looks particularly impressive.

Remember, it always pays to finish with some high drama and possible amusement.

Funboard Freestyle

A much more specialized technique is 'sinker freestyle', which is reserved for the strong winds needed to sail a sinker. A handful of sailors have taken the time to evolve sinker tacks, helicopters and 360s, and these tricks can be used in a waveriding routine, which is the equivalent of freestyle on the waves, marked in the same way by judges watching from the shore.

Above: When you start to learn to railride it's a lot easier to keep one foot on the daggerboard. Remember to protect your shins for kneeling on the rails. They are very hard on bare skin, and if you're not experienced like Dee Caldwell it's easy to end up with a mass of bruises. Dee is dipping the stern for some rock 'n' roll.

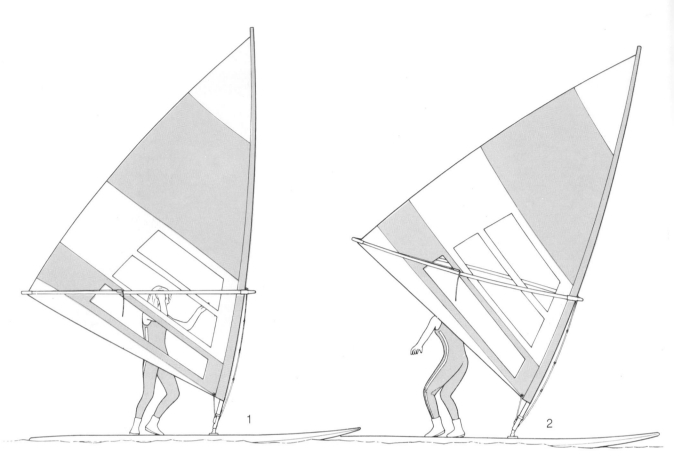

Duck Track Pirouette

This one combines several tricks that can be done while the board is flat on the water – as yet no one has managed to do it on the rail!

Sail along close hauled, but get up a good turn of speed before you go into your tack. Rake the rig aft in the conventional manner. Wait until the nose of the board starts to pass through the eye of the wind – and at this point forget all you know and

start learning all over again.

Pause, let go with your mast hand, and then throw the rig well forward with your sheet hand (**1**). Let go of the wishbone altogether, and duck under the foot of the sail

---

Ladies' Tricks

Ladies can do some tricks which men will find pretty hard to handle, mainly because of the different way in which we are put together.

A windsurfer is an ideal platform for the splits, but you should know how to do it on dry land before giving it a go on the sea.

As with most tricks, it's easiest to start on a reach – it gives you plenty of power and enough latitude for recovery if things go wrong.

Head up on to a close reach, and begin to slide your front foot forward, followed by your back foot. If the wishbone is high you may have to drop your hands on to the mast and the foot of the sail.

The board will start to head up

into the wind, particularly if it is blowing hard, so you need to get back on to your feet fairly rapidly.

Somersault

The somersault through the wishbone is a good way to finish off your routine, though if you land up on your feet still sailing, you have to think of another dismount in double quick time.

You really need a minimum of Force 3 to make it worthwhile, and the windier it is, the more spectacular the trick will be.

The theory is simple. You sail on a close reach, and when you're ready, sheet out a little to give you enough room to kick up and go through the wishbone feet first. You've got to kick hard and go into

a semi-tuck position to fit through. Also it's got to be the one and only. If you go at it in a half-hearted manner, you'll end up without the impetus to get you through, and the rig will collapse down around your head.

Combinations

Big freestyle events normally include competitions for combinations. These can include two people on one board; two people on two boards sailing along together; even more than two people on one or more boards (trying not to sink them); and two people on a tandem.

None of these are as serious as the regular one-up routine, but the two-up tricks are always good for

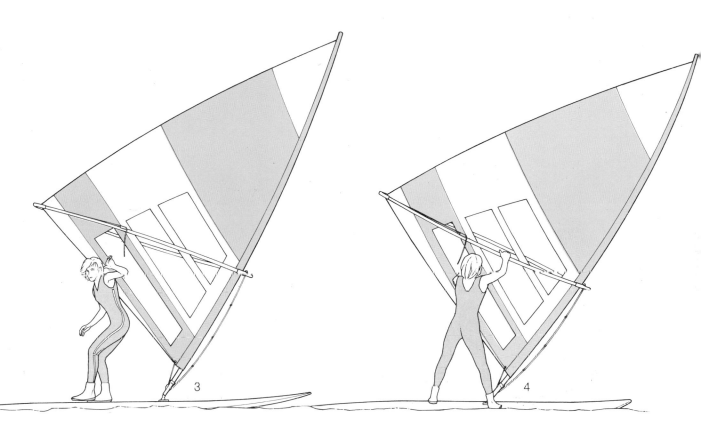

3

4

(2), ready to grasp the wishbone on the new tack (3) first with your mast hand (4), and then with your sheet hand.

Until you've got the hang of it, it's easier to grab hold of the foot of the sail with one hand as you duck under it – otherwise you're likely to lose the rig altogether.

That was a basic duck tack, but when you're really good you can combine it with the pirouette shown here – rather than simply ducking under the foot of the sail, you pirouette through 360 degrees while you're doing it. Conditions need to be right so that the rig is not blown away from you.

laughs, and are now getting established in the calendar. They tend to attract either a boyfriend/girlfriend duo, or a father and young son. The participants tend to enjoy the first, while the second has the great advantage of one member of the team being unusually light and agile, but with some strength ready to hand if it's needed.

Final Points
1. Prepare the board thoroughly.
2. Master each trick – on the

Right: Back-to-the-sail head dip. The sailor holds on to the rig, but he's facing backwards. It's not as difficult as it looks. However he makes it a little more difficult with a head dip in the water.

Left: A triple team with two boards performs a complex ascent of the rig – it helps when a couple of them are very small, very light, and very agile. This is more exhibitionist freestyle than anything done to a precise competition routine, but it is probably a good way to keep a family amused.

beach, in shallow water, in deep water, in light, medium, and strong winds, and in waves.

3. Work out a routine which is decided upon in advance.

4. Ensure that the tricks flow into one another, and keep you and your board within a relatively small area – you don't want to sail off miles from both judges and spectators.

5. Amuse the audience, and try to look happy.

6. Try to develop your own new variation on a trick.

7. Don't be psyched out by the routines of the competitors who come before you.

8. End your routine with a dramatic flourish – but don't just jump in the water.

Pirouette

During a perfect pirouette the rig hardly moves even though it is unsupported.

To do it this way the board needs to be moving quite fast through the water, and a Force 2 wind is ideal. If the wind is any stronger, there is a danger that the rig will be blown out of your reach by a gust, while if the wind is any lighter, the rig will simply fall over into the water.

It's easiest to do it on a very broad reach, so that when you turn you don't get tangled with the rig and knock it to one side – for this reason you should also keep your arms well in to your body and spin on one foot in a very tight circle.

In the illustration, the sailor has just let go of the rig, and is spinning

anti-clockwise on the ball of her foot (**1**). She turns full circle in a matter of a couple of seconds, ready to grab the wishbone (**2**) and keep sailing (**3**). If you don't get dizzy, you could perform several pirouettes like this in swift succession – they are one of the most graceful manoeuvres in a freestyle routine.

Windsurfing Feats

The flamboyant Baron Arnaud de Rosnay once said that anyone considering windsurfing across the Atlantic had no idea what was involved – it just could not be done.

However, within a year a French airline pilot had done just that, windsurfing the breadth of the Atlantic without leaving his board.

Christian Marty had planned the trip for two years. During that time he took extended leave from Air France to prepare himself. He studied psychology, biology, and climatology; took up cycling, jogging, walking, and hanging from trees (to build up his arm muscles!) and set a couple of first time windsurfing records by sailing from the French Riviera to Corsica, and going around the island of Guadeloupe in 51 hours non-stop.

The trip was budgeted at £100,000, paid for by Marty's three sponsors: the magazine VSD; the radio station Antenne 2; and the board manufacturer Sodim, who provided Marty with his Oversea board, a new 350 cm strong wind design that was selected as being easy to sail and fast in a variety of conditions.

Marty had planned to sail from Dakar in French West Africa to Martinique in the West Indies. He would not leave his board during the crossing, which he estimated at between 28–40 days, and would be accompanied all the way across by a support ship, the 70 foot ketch *Assiduous*, crewed by 12 of his friends. They would bring him his food via the yacht's tender, and at night would prepare him for sleep.

In order to live on his board 24 hours a day for a month, Marty had hit on an ingenious system. He would de-rig his board and hand the whole lot over to the waiting crew in the tender, who would then pass him an inflatable collar with which to encircle his board – the idea was that he could lie down and sleep inside it quite comfortably. He would then rig a short mast with

Above: Christian Marty had three inflatable support boats, which brought him all he needed from *Assiduous*, including his thrice daily meals, and gear for settling down for the night.

a flashlight and radar reflector to make sure he stayed in contact with *Assiduous*. He also planned to fly a small staysail which would pull him along at night, but abandoned this idea as he felt it was cheating.

Marty was equipped with an immense variety of sails, all coloured apple green which was supposed to be easy to spot at sea without being a strain on Marty's eyes (though it turned out that *Assiduous* frequently had difficulty finding him). Just to be safe he took three identical suits of nine sails each, ranging from three to nine square metres.

During the crossing, the predictable Trade Wind was astern, and he devised a sailing system with a harness, an inflatable seat, and a double wishbone, which would allow him to sail sitting down in a comfortable position. Initially he used a high seat, but as the crossing progressed he made it lower and lower until eventually he was sitting on the board.

Departure

Marty left Dakar on November 28th 1981. This was the time of year when he could expect consistently safe conditions in the latitudes he was crossing. The Trades would blow from the North-East at between 15 and 25 knots, giving him a fair wind and a comfortable sea temperature – Doctor Bombard had planned his famous journey in a rubber liferaft along much the same principles.

Marty ran into trouble almost immediately. On the first night he capsized several times while he was sleeping, and was thrown into the water. This was to happen again later on the voyage, but initially he was able to overcome the problem by lowering the safety lamp on the mast until it did not interfere with the balance of the board, and attaching a couple of ship's fenders either side to make it more stable. With a set-up like this he was able to sleep amidst five metre waves when the wind blew up to 32 knots on the third night.

Five days and 150 miles out of Dakar, it was *Assiduous* that ran into trouble, rather than Marty. Her rudder was damaged and the only option was to put back for repairs, before the team could set out once again after a 10 day delay.

The delay forced Marty to change his plans. Most of the crew of *Assiduous* had voluntarily taken time off from their regular jobs, and for everyone time was at a premium. Therefore, he decided to go for the nearest point on the other side of the Atlantic, Cayenne in French Guiana – it was almost 1000 miles closer than Martinique, but still 2400 miles and more than one month distant.

Right: Marty windsurfed eight hours a day, using a secondary wishbone so that he could sit down. As the trip progressed his seat got lower and lower, until he was sitting on the board.

The Crossing

Once underway again, things went well for Marty. He broke the 1000 miles barrier after 17 days, having established a regimen of windsurfing eight hours a day; sleeping six to eight hours a day; and eating three main meals a day.

His food revolved around dried fruit and tea for breakfast; and red meat, vegetables, Gruyère cheese and noodles for both lunch and dinner. On New Year's Eve this diet was radically improved, and *Assiduous* brought him a punch made from the remnants of their rum, plus sausage cocktails, Nantua *quenelles* with American sauce, roast pork with prunes, and apricot pie. At midnight this was followed by champagne and fireworks (distress rockets) let off by the crew!

As on the first attempt it was *Assiduous* that ran into more problems than Marty. First the crew was seasick, and then the generator broke down. Since they had also managed to flatten the ship's batteries, they were unable to start the engine, and had no light, no radio, no satellite navigation, and nothing to run the galley. For a month this forced them to live in a shambles, with all the cooking for 13 men being done on a small single gas ring in the forecabin. This carried on until eventually one of them hit on the idea of starting the engine with a diving compressor.

Marty carried on regardless, logging 70 and more miles a day on his eight hour shifts 'like someone who has a job'.

His morale stayed consistently high, but was nearly broken by a narrow escape from drowning and increasingly unfavourable currents as he neared the South American coastline.

The near drowning was one of those little incidents in which the

At night Marty would surround his board with an inflatable collar, with a couple of fenders for stability in rough seas.

situation rapidly gets worse. He had capsized whilst sleeping several times before, and it happened once again. He had also lost two sleeping bags this way, and when he saw the third one floating two metres away from him, he tried to get it. He moved away slightly from his board, which was on its side, when it suddenly righted itself. Immediately it began to be carried away by the current faster than Marty could swim – with each stroke, his hand hit the water a foot behind the board and he was unable to catch it. He remembered those moments at the Press Conference a month later. 'I fought for eight minutes. I understood then that I was going to die. This may seem funny but I thought of my children and my wife

Rough and cold weather on the east side of the Atlantic. Until the last days, the wind seldom deserted Marty.

who awaited me at Cayenne. I stopped swimming, and I screamed. By an incredible stroke of good fortune my crew was passing nearby at that moment. They returned me to my board, 300 metres away – that, I will never forget.'

His team had seen nothing. When the board capsized, it was hidden by the swell, and when it came back into view, it had righted itself – they had no reason to assume that anything was amiss.

And if they had not heard him? There is no doubt that Marty would have been lost. Everything designed to help him survive if he became separated from *Assiduous* – VHF/ADF radio, flares, food, water purification system, and compass – was on his board, and he

would never have been seen again.

After this, Marty tethered himself to the board. Progress became slower and slower as they moved through wind and sea conditions that became variable and unpredictable near the Equator. As they got closer to the coast, the powerful Amazonian current set them off course – they were not equipped with the local tide charts.

Eventually, after a week of battling with the Amazon, Marty completed his journey. On 18th January 1982 he surfed the bar at Kourou near Cayenne at 13 knots, and drove up on to the beach.

He had windsurfed the Atlantic, covering 2400 miles of open ocean. He had not left his board for 37 days, 16 hours, and 14 minutes.

Baron Arnaud de Rosnay

Baron Arnaud de Rosnay is a very different animal from the self-effacing Christian Marty.

Born into the wealth of a Mauritian sugar plantation, with French and Russian parents (his father is a painter) de Rosnay is a windsurfing entrepreneur/explorer, always determined to hit the headlines, and always successful in doing so.

First Feats

The Baron has always been an excellent publicist for his feats, which began when he 'landsurfed' the Sahara in 1979.

He had invented what he called a Speed Sail – a sort of windsurfer on wheels looking like a nine foot long skateboard – and wanted to prove its prowess. To do so, he 'landsurfed' 220 miles from the borders of Mauritania to Dakar, with a jeep (carrying a driver, three guides, a photographer and a journalist) in attendance. Sponsorship was provided by the French Channel 2 TV, VSD magazine, and Lacoste clothing.

The Baron's second feat followed close after in the same year. On August 31st he windsurfed across the shortest aquatic distance between Russia and America – the Bering Straits.

In fact he had to go a little further. Sixty-five miles is the direct distance, but that culminates in a 1000 foot high sheer rock face, so he had to cover another 20 miles to find a rather more hospitable landfall.

The conditions were not good. The Straits are only navigable for three summer months every year (the rest of the time it is frozen) and even then the temperature is a mere four degrees Centigrade with strong winds being the norm.

The board chosen by the Baron was a Windsurfer Rocket, dressed up to look like a TC39, which his sponsors, Ten Cate, were marketing. With him he took his passport, $500 in cash, flares, and chocolate – but no sanction from either the US or Russian governments.

Half way over, a Russian destroyer took up station to escort him to their side. It took eight hours to complete the crossing, he lost his gloves, and when he arrived he was so tired and cold that he fell off several times trying to get back to the ship and security, and had to be picked up by a launch.

The fact that he had entered Russia illegally was overlooked. He was entertained to caviar and vodka

Christian Marty dressed for any weather, with a look of indefatigable determination like Lawrence of Arabia.

by the ship's captain, and was then flown to Moscow and on to Paris, where he could begin the planning of his third major feat.

The Pacific

In 1980 the Baron made his most controversial voyage.

He intended windsurfing across the Pacific, from the Marquesas to the islands of Hawaii, retracing the original Polynesian route of discovery. He would be accompanied by a support boat, and like Marty he would never leave his board.

The trip took six months to prepare. He had a specially designed windsurfer which had an inflatable neoprene 'doughnut' round its circumference. He could stand up and windsurf by day, while at night he laid the rig across his board with floats attached to either end of the mast to make the whole contraption into a trimaran. He could then blow up his doughnut, and snuggle down inside it while a parakite pulled him along at 3–5 knots, with the Trade Winds behind. The whole apparatus weighed just over 100 pounds, and was 12 foot long with a 15 foot beam and a 10 inch freeboard.

He had chosen the weather carefully. No storms, and the Trades giving between 17 and 22 knots by day and night. By day he would stand and windsurf, while by night the parakite would continue to power him in the right direction.

All the preparation came to nought when de Rosnay set out on 29th August. His support craft made a bare six knots while he was sailing at 12, and he found that he had to stop and wait for her to catch up every half hour.

The attempt was abandoned, and they had no option but to turn back. However de Rosnay would not give up his plan. Since the authorities refused to allow him to leave without a support craft, he decided to give them the slip, and left once again, alone, and in the middle of the night.

His plans had changed. He would head South rather than North – his main intention seems to have been to cover as much of the open Pacific as possible, with the Tuamotus group of islands being his destination.

Once under way the board and the parakite worked well, but the problems multiplied. He had reckoned on sheltering from the sun behind the sail, but with the effect of salt water he soon had boils on every joint. His lethal-sounding remedy was to windsurf nude and in the full sun for two days, 'to burn off the infection'. From then on he wore a loose fitting Helly Hansen suit, jumping in the water once an hour to cool off.

He was attacked by a couple of sharks, and lived in constant fear of encountering a 10 footer. Nor was his navigation very successful. There was at least a six foot swell, and if he wanted to use his sextant he had to go through the rigmarole of turning his board into a stable trimaran, and then disassembling it. This took a total of 40 minutes, so rather than get his mid-day sight, he put the sextant in its box and sent if off on its way across the ocean. From then on he navigated by compass and dead reckoning – ie estimating his course, and how fast he was travelling.

After sunburn, sharks, and navigation, his fourth great problem was food and water. He had reckoned on being at sea for a week, and had left with one and a half gallons of water, some dates and nuts, and

The great windsurfing pioneer Baron Arnaud de Rosnay was imbued with a delightful air of 19th eccentricity.

NASA survival tablets – he was later to say, 'they are very terrible to eat – like foie gras surrounded by chocolate'.

He was drinking fresh and sea water in a mix of 2:1 as the NASA nutritionists recommended, but after six days there was very little water left. He had two solar stills, but couldn't use them while he was sailing, and hopefully getting closer to land. A couple of rain showers helped, but after 12 days all the water was gone, and de Rosnay had to abandon sailing, and just lie down and let the parakite pull the board while the stills slowly made him some water.

He was lucky. The following day he found land and he found people. He had reached the Island of Ahe, one of the Tuamotus group, after 750 miles of open water, and had just survived.

However, he was even luckier to survive the fury of the French government and the indignation of the French press. During his fortnight at sea the French navy had expended a great deal of their taxpayers' money on a fruitless search for him, and had then declared him missing presumed dead. When he eventually made it back to Paris the French press largely lambasted him as a fraud, and he spent a great deal of time trying to persuade them otherwise. The Russians signed a document saying that he had indeed crossed the Bering Straits, and eventually he and his own people were able to make their peace.

Postscript

Of course a showman never lies down, and a year later the Baron was in the news again. On one side

Baron Arnaud de Rosnay prior to racing Ken Winner across the English Channel for $5000. They both had to be rescued by helicopter, and they both lost their boards.

of the world he was busy organizing a professional 'Speed Crossing' between the Hawaiian islands of Maui (his adopted home) and Molokai, while on the other he had to be rescued from the middle of the English Channel after challenging Ken Winner to a race from Britain to France. The prize was $5000 – and neither of them won it!

In the summer of 1982 the Baron had another go at the English Channel, and broke the record sailing from France to England, and then back again. By this time he had become fascinated by speed, and was a regular competitor at the major speed events in Weymouth and Brest. He proved his ability by being one of the four fastest men in the world, while his wife Jenna became Ladies' Speed Champion in 1982 and again in 1984.

Arnaud restarted his crossings in earnest when he windsurfed across the Straits of Gibraltar in December 1983. He followed this with a crossing between Miami and Cuba in early 1984, and a couple of months later windsurfed the Sakhalin Straits which divide Japan and the USSR.

His last great crossing was to be from mainland China to the nationalist Chinese island of Taiwan – two territories which were theoretically 'at war'. He set out on 24th November 1984, and has never been seen again.

No one knows what happened. Some believe it could have been pirates or a trigger happy soldier, but the most likely explanation is that a windsurfing accident separated Arnaud from his board, claiming the life of windsurfing's most flamboyant ambassador.

Chronology

1979
February. Ken Winner windsurfs 100 miles along the Florida coast in 6 hours 49 minutes.
August. Baron Arnaud de Rosnay windsurfs across the Bering Straits from Alaska to Siberia. He covers 85 miles in 8 hours without assistance.
November. Sergio Ferrero of Italy windsurfs 150 miles from Ibiza to Barcelona.
December. Frederic Beauchêne of France windsurfs in hops around Cape Horn, with a support team and two inflatable boats.

Christian Marty (no doubt taking advantage of an airline employee's cheap flight) windsurfs 100 miles from Guadeloupe to Martini-

que, in preparation for his 1982 Atlantic crossing.

1980
June. Christian Marty windsurfs 105 miles from Nice to Corsica.
September. Baron Arnaud de Rosnay covers 750 miles of the Pacific in 13 days unassisted. He is not popular with the French navy.
October. Anne Gardner and Jack Wood windsurf across the 70 miles of the world's highest stretch of water, Lake Titicaca in South America.

1981
September. An English team windsurfs around the UK on a Sea Panther board.
December. Frederic Giraldi of France windsurfs from the Canaries to Guadaloupe. He intended staying on his board all the way across, but resorted to sleeping on his support boat each night.

1982
January. Christian Marty windsurfs the Atlantic from Africa to America without leaving his board.
June. Prince Sergio Ferrero windsurfs from Las Palmas to Barbados with the aid of a support boat.

Fred Beauchêne silhouetted against Cape Horn – a unique and solitary achievement.

1983
January. Arnaud de Rosnay sets out to windsurf the 3000 kilometres of the Caribbean island chain in 30 days. The attempt is abandoned after he has sailed 1000 kilometres.
December. Arnaud de Rosnay windsurfs from Morocco to Spain.

1984
January. Arnaud de Rosnay windsurfs from Miami (USA) to Cuba.
July. Stephan Peyron (France) windsurfs non-stop for 70 hours, covering 506 kilometres.

Arnaud de Rosnay windsurfs from the Japanese island of Hokkaido to the Russian military island of Sakhalin.
May–July. Tim Batstone windsurfs round the UK with a support boat. He completes 1777 miles in 70 days, starting and finishing at the Thames.

1985
July. Frederic Beauchêne and Thierry Caroni windsurf the Atlantic on a specially designed tandem. Their crossing takes 38 days.

New Ideas

The windsurfing concept isn't just limited to use on water, and even when it is, it can find some strange new directions, as the picture opposite shows.

Windsurfing got popular about the same time as skateboarding though happily it's here to stay, rather than being just a short-lived craze. However the principles behind the two sports are similar – speed, sensation, and balance – and in the past 10 years various 'landsurfers' have been produced which combine the windsurfer rig with a skateboard or something similar.

The most basic combination of a mast foot on a standard skateboard proved unworkable – too difficult to control, with far too much strain on the tiny wheels – and the manufacturers who entered this field were forced to seek a considerably more sophisticated design solution.

In most cases the basic principles of a skateboard have been retained. The board should be steered by banking it, and this turns the wheels on the damped steering system.

The variations are in the size and shape of the board and its wheels. Obviously a light board with small wheels giving minimum skin resistance will travel very fast, but will only do so on a perfect surface such as tarmac, and by virtue of its size will be very difficult to sail.

A larger board will take more wind to get moving and will build up speed more slowly, but is bound to be easier to control and will be far more at home when the surface is of variable solidity, as on a beach. The softer the sand, the broader the wheels need to be, and footballs mounted on bearings have proved very successful. Taken to its limit, Baron Arnaud de Rosnay's Speed Sail (see pages 154–157) with which he windsurfed the Sahara was a nine foot long skateboard with 4 + 4 wheels – he added the second set to make eight in all for very soft sand.

Sailing a Landsurfer

The most obvious difference between landsurfing and windsurfing is falling off. It's hard, and if it's on tarmac it will be very hard and you'll be going very fast. Obviously you have to wear all the skateboarding gear – crash hat, knee and elbow pads – and take great care not to break your neck.

The technique is also different. Compared to water the surface is smooth and there is far less skin friction. You travel a lot faster in the same amount of wind, and consequently the 'apparent wind' changes direction very rapidly. Once you build up speed, you always need to sheet the sail in tight, much as on a short funboard, and a high aspect rig of around 4.5 sq m is generally ideal.

On most landsurfers, raking the rig fore and aft plays a minor part in steering. Instead, the board is steered by banking it, which turns the axles of the front wheels. Gybing is relatively easy, but when it comes to tacking you need to take great care. On a windsurfer you come to a virtual dead stop as the nose passes through the eye of the wind. However on a landsurfer you carry on moving with little loss of speed. You tack through an arc, and it's unnerving when you move round the front of the mast to change sides, facing backwards and still travelling at 20 miles per hour!

Commercially the most successful landsurfer is de Rosnay's Speed Sail design which has a class association, and World, European and National Championships. These are held at venues with hard sand or dried salt beds, and feature pentathlon style competition with triangle racing, freestyle, slalom, marathon and speed trials. In the right conditions they are capable of over 70 kph, and a special prototype claimed to achieve a speed of 139 kph during the summer of 1985, which sounded like a very dangerous undertaking!

On Ice and Snow

If a windsurfer rig can be used on land it can obviously be used on ice, and the Russians are forerunners in this part of the game. They favour small boards of around two-and-a-half foot maximum length fitted with ice runners, and often use solid wing rigs to cope with the immense speeds they run at. Fifty mph+ is the norm, so it's not a sport for the fainthearted.

Using a windsurfer rig on snow is somewhat different, as there is much more skin friction and obviously the speeds are lower. However, enthusiasts in North America and Scandinavia have successfully mated rigs with skis and toboggans in much the same fashion.

Hydrofoils

The idea of the hydrofoil is that once a craft reaches an initial speed, it will 'lift out' and stand up on its foils, which have a far smaller wetted area than the hull itself.

The principle has been tried with limited success on windsurfers. They have problems reaching the required speed to 'lift out' due to the drag of the submerged foils, and then when the board does lift out, it becomes very difficult to control.

An interesting tandem-hydrofoil-proa was designed to overcome these problems – tandem for power; proa outrigger for stability –

Jim Drake is generally credited as the man who invented it all (see pages 12–13) and at Hawaii in 1982 he looked ready to start it all again, with a rig that would certainly beat the patent, and looked as though it had been developed from a hang-glider. The locals tried it hooked on and hanging in, but the likeable and easy-going Mr Drake had his tongue firmly in his cheek all the time. We'll have to wait and see what he comes up with in the future.

but met with limited success. It was named 'Sweeny' after its designer, Mike Todd.

Different Rigs

The windsurfer rig as developed and patented by Hoyle Schweitzer has remained much the same. The shaping and materials used may have improved, but it is still recognizably the 20 year old original.

Most of the rigs which are obviously rather different have been dreamt up by or resurrected by 'patent beaters'. Thus Newman Darby's square-rigger type of windsurfer sail was proudly held up to the German courts as 'prior art' – ie someone else had invented the windsurfer before Schweitzer. This attempt was unsuccessful, but other people set out to design rigs specifically to circumvent the patent. Such rigs do the same job while wriggling round the intricacies of the law.

We have therefore seen some very odd variations on the conventional wishbone. There was the straight sided one that was popular in the UK for a few years; another that looked like a hair pin with curly sides; and a single straight boom that sliced the sail in half. Peter Chilvers, the man who was held by the British courts to have sailed a 'sailboard' before Schweitzer, developed a rig based on this principle, claiming its superiority to the conventional rig. However there was no sign of it being a commercial success.

A further answer to the patent question was a four sided 'quadsail' (another British invention) which allowed the wishbone to be attached to the leading edge of the sail without touching the mast. Like most of the other 'patent beaters' it worked reasonably well, without demonstrating any particular superiority over the Schweitzer rig, and once the patent question was decided the development of these strange rigs ceased.

Above: The renaissance of the skateboard! Some enthusiasts perform freestyle and slalom with a windsurfer rig on a skateboard. Surprisingly high speeds can be achieved, but with hard landings it's not for the fainthearted.

Left: Speed Sail in action. It can perform funboard manoeuvres at breathtaking speeds in very light winds.

Where It's At

Windsurfing is best experienced when the weather and water are warm, and when there's a good breeze. For those who haven't tried it, windsurfing without a wetsuit is a thousand times better than cold, clammy, constricting rubber.

There are now holiday packages for windsurfers available in most of the desirable corners of the world. These vary from the very simple and very cheap, to the sophisticated and very expensive. Either way, you should check out whether it's a holiday that just happens to include windsurfing, or one that has been specifically designed around the needs of the sport – otherwise, you may be disappointed.

Occasionally you will be expected to take your own boards and equipment, but usually the board at least will be provided. In this case it is important to check that the sort of boards you like sailing are available, and just how much use of them will be included in the cost of the package. Remember that being saddled with some ancient board is almost as bad as twiddling your thumbs on the beach while someone hogs the one you want to try.

Holidays are excellent for learning windsurfing. Two uninterrupted weeks of perfect conditions are enough to get anyone past the basics, but you should ensure the teaching is to the standard you require. It is best by far if a proper course is on offer which will give you a recognized national certificate. In some countries you may actually need this certificate before they allow you to go windsurfing as a requirement for insurance.

Some holidays also cater for advanced learning – ie getting you through the Force 4+ barrier and on as far as wave jumping techniques, with some tuition thrown in. This will enable you to try sailing in more difficult conditions without having to buy expensive specialist equipment.

Right: Florida in the the Gulf of Mexico. As a simple rule of thumb, anywhere with nice big palm trees is OK when it comes to windsurfing – anywhere with sharks is not so good.

Below: The Island of Hydra in the Aegean Sea off Greece. Lovely and warm, and in the hot summer months the Meltemi is a reliable afternoon wind, blowing at Force 4 or 5 every day. Hydra hosted the Windsurfer World Championship in the autumn of 1979 — at that time of the year the weather was unfortunately less pleasant.

Regattas

Regatta sailing is a great way to travel. Most of the major class associations run their European and World events in exotic places, and have special cheap packages which enable competitors to turn them into two week family holidays.

You will invariably find that boards and rigs are provided gratis or for a nominal fee by the one-design associations. After the event is over this equipment is normally sold off very cheap for those who want to take advantage of it.

The package will also include travel, hotel, and a succession of parties, barbecues, discos, etc, making the cost almost inclusive.

Sun Care

Many windsurfers live in northern climes and are not used to fair weather sailing. Therefore some sensible precautions need to be taken.

Windsurfing is a great way to get a suntan. The sail reflects the bright light (if you want to get really brown, a white sail is *de rigeur*) which also bounces back off the water, while the wind keeps you cool. But it is also a great way to get burnt, and it is no good ruining your holiday by needing a week's recovery after one day's wind-surfing.

If it's really hot, protect your body, and it may be advisable to wear a hat as well. Most important of all, don't burn your feet. Standing on a gleaming white board with your feet half submerged can lead to critical sunburn, and you should either wear some footwear, or a waterproof sun tan cream that has a powerful screen. Some brands are very effective. It takes a long time

Just look at that surf! This is Hookipa Beach on the island of Maui, one of the Hawaiian group. If anything it's rated more highly than Diamond Head on the nearby island of Oahu.

Transporting a Board

When you go off to your favourite hotspot, you may well prefer to take your own board rather than risk hiring.

Most of the airlines will carry boards, but just how easy this is varies from place to place and from airline to airline. It used to be the case that you could simply turn up at the airport with your board under your arm, and they would take it as part of the baggage allowance.

However, now that windsurfing is a lot more popular, you stand a pretty good chance of getting turned away at the check-in. You should always check with the airline in advance what facilities they have for boards, and then you won't be disappointed. Some will still take them as baggage, while others want a fat fee for taking them cargo (and one month in advance). Hopefully the rest have special deals available.

Take care when you trust your board to the tender mercies of the airport ground staff. To them it's a big solid lump, and if you want it to arrive in one piece, make sure it's well wrapped in expanded polythene sheeting with all the accessories taped firmly to the board. Also make sure you understand the insurance liability before you travel.

Europe

Most Europeans head for the Mediterranean, where the summer guarantees sun, even if the wind isn't more forthcoming.

Generally, the further east you go, the more reliable the wind will be. In the hottest months the Greek Meltemi blows up every afternoon, reaching Force 4 or more and blowing steadily until the evening. It is predictable and you know what to expect, but further west the wind can strike with unexpected severity. Any sailor who has tried the coastal area around Marseilles knows how quickly the Mistral transforms the placid Mediterranean, and it is very easy to get caught out.

Further north, the great Euro-

A Thai duet on two Thai boards in Israel! This is Nahariya, just near the border on the Israeli Mediterranean coast, during the Open Class World Championship in 1980. The competitors were protected by gunboats!

pean windsurfing centre is Lake Garda near Milan in Italy. Every summer weekend it's liable to be saturated by around 6000 windsurfers, the majority of whom are German, Austrian, and, of course, Italian.

They come for the thermal winds that are caused by the mountains that encircle the lake. Every morning there's the Vento which seldom blows more than Force 3 and is ideal for beginners, while every afternoon the Ora takes over for the better sailors with Force 5–8.

North again, and the West Country of England has the reputation for the best wave sailing in Europe – but it's not reliable.

The Atlantic
The Canary Islands are considered good strong wind/sun areas, benefiting from Trade Winds all the year round, and at their best in the summer.

On the opposite side of the Atlantic, the West Indies are just a little bit further south, so they get rather more sun with the same predictable wind pattern. The French islands (Guadeloupe, Martinique, etc) are all well known for windsurfing.

USA
The warm weather states of California and Florida are both popular, with San Francisco Bay having a particularly good summertime reputation, even though the water stays cold. For winter sun, visits over the Mexican border are recommended, with Baja and Cancun both being good.

Hawaii is, of course, the American Number One, whether it's winter or summer. It may be expensive (to get to and live in), overcrowded (on the capital island of Oahu at least), and have a wind that isn't always predictable, but it still continues to attract the stars due to its excellent waves.

Australia
Australia now has some of the world's best strong wind sailing, while a short hop to Thailand's Siam Cup must be the best way to spend each Christmas (although the wind can be unpredictable). In fact the list is endless. Wherever there's sun, sea, and a good wind, there will be windsurfers.

Guadeloupe in the French West Indies was the venue of the 1979 Open Class World Championship, and is pretty desirable by any standards. The food is better than on the British or American islands, and the girls are a lot prettier, although it does tend to be more expensive. Martinique is its smart neighbour.

Photography with Alastair Black

Surely one of the sporting world's most spectacular subjects, windsurfing has to be also one of the most challenging. As a professional photographer I have to be armed with every available weapon for this challenge or I cannot hope to cover the full range of options available. But virtually every reader is going to be an amateur with a limited budget for photo equipment, so how can I be helpful and at the same time practical within the limitations?

Probably the most helpful suggestion will be – think carefully about each picture. Do not just point and shoot. It is so easy to look with your eyes, then lift up the camera, peer through the viewfinder, and see what you want to see – not what is really there. Even after years of looking through finders I still have to tell myself positively to see the image critically, to remember how small that sailboard in the centre really is in relation to the total picture area, to spot the distractions around it, to think of the lighting situation as it will affect the result. And above all, not to take a photo if the result will be dull and uninteresting.

Of course, what is dull to one person can be fascinating to another, so I should not really discourage any kind of image creation. Certainly there is no better way to learn than by making mistakes!

Equipment

It really is an impossibility to produce any passable photograph with a commonly used snapshot camera intended for family snaps of the baby and Aunt Ethel. These are ingenious, clever pieces of equipment, but simply lack lenses of adequate focal length even to remotely fill sufficient space in the picture area with a sailboard. There could be the odd occasion when an opportunity comes along for the distance to be short enough. But on the whole, forget it.

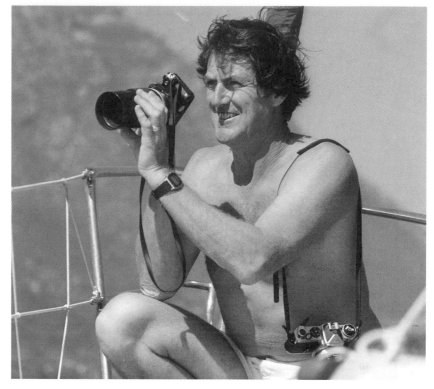

To begin producing good windsurfing photos, a single lens reflex camera with interchangeable lenses is essential, and it should not only offer automatic exposure which can be invaluable at the right time, but manual over-ride also. There are plenty of makes which are adequate, reliable and easy to use. No particular recommendations here but all the well-known names produce good models.

A zoom lens, from 70–200 mm focal length or thereabouts, will be invaluable, as it offers more scope for 'filling the frame' from varying distances. If a shorter focal length zoom, say 35–70 mm is added, then you have no excuses – well, not many.

The greatest difference between an amateur and a professional photographer is not necessarily the ability of the latter to produce good photos. It is the fact that the pro *must* produce good work each and every time, plus enough of it to satisfy the many markets waiting to

Above: Alastair Black threw up his living as a dentist to become an international yachting photographer. He never looked back.

use it. So, as amateurs, it's a piece of cake. You have nothing to lose, can take chances, try any ideas and all you lose is a bit of film.

Now for a few guidelines on some basic essentials. I shall assume the reader has a knowledge of the mechanics of photography because this is not the place to start explaining about focal lengths, f-stops, film speeds and all the details involved with understanding how to generate reasonable photos. If that knowledge is absent, there are countless 'How To' photo books available, which will provide the necessary background information.

Right: The end of the day, using a UV filter which is enough to make the orange light at that time even stronger.

Films

I would suggest you use only reversal film, ie slides. Like most professionals I am a Kodachrome addict – generally 64 ASA – because it is so sharp, has good colour and can be processed anywhere. Black and white loses all the potential of colour. Colour negative film can only produce prints. Slides offer everything – good prints can now be made easily from them – they are necessary for all the repro-duction you see in magazines and books – and they can be projected on to a screen. Another advantage is that every frame can be easily seen to compare your work without having to obtain a print first.

Using colour calls for sunshine shooting, because there is little that is more boring that a white sailed windsurfer on a grey and windless day. For years I have campaigned against these dull, tedious, drab, white sails in what is essentially a bright, extrovert, exciting sport.

So try to save your film and efforts for a sunny day preferably with a brisk wind. But even when winds are gentle there is plenty you can produce. Late in the day, in particular, is best. From late afternoon on to sunset in the summertime can produce much warmer colours, and if the sun is low it makes a wonderful background to shoot into – lots of sparkle on the water with that golden orb itself

making the perfect backdrop for a windsurfer (even one with a white sail).

When using colour film at sea it is necessary to use an ultraviolet or skylight filter to cut down the overall blue cast in these conditions. A skylight has more red in its effect, so outside the couple of hours around midday the clouds can become a little too pink and the warming-up effect a bit excessive as sunset draws nearer. For that reason I use U.V. constantly, and even it can turn an evening scene into an orange glow that is much more vivid than the eye can perceive.

If using B.W. film, a yellow or orange filter will add greatly to the contrast between white sails or clouds and sky.

For really strong colour effects, a polarizing filter used to its maximum potential will bring out all the colours with an unreal vividness.

Some people like this but I seldom use polarizers as the results can be too unnatural – and you lose two stops in speed because of these filters' light absorbing nature.

Nowadays there are also hundreds of 'creative' filters in a variety of systems. Several can be useful in windsurfing photography but in general no filter will make a silk purse out of a sow's ear, so if your basic shot is second rate it will still be second rate 'with filter effect'.

Remember again – think before you shoot.

★　　★　　★

Having covered what can be in and what can be on the camera, it is time to consider where it is going to be when the pictures are being made. Ignoring aerial photography, which is strictly professional, three other possible bases for your camera exist: On the land. On the water. In the water.

Above: If this had been taken from the other side of the windsurfers, the effect would have been flat and uninteresting – always think about how a different position has a different image.

Right: Keep your eyes open for the unexpected. No photo skill is needed apart from observation and the ability to focus quickly when using a telephoto lens – and remember the exposure.

On the Land

Obviously this limits the angles. All the action is going on outside your control and pictures have to be made within these limitations.

If your stretch of land is on the south of the water, then all the photos are going to have normal 'over-the-shoulder' lighting and there is no chance of sparkly backlit water photos.

If it is to the west or east of the water then the lighting will vary according to the time of day, so if sailing is going on all day and you can choose when to shoot, think about when conditions may be best or when they provide the effects you most want.

If your base faces south over the water, most times are going to offer the chance for backlit photos only. This is pictorially the most attractive, but it means that the subject's face and the details are usually in shadow so there will be problems if the object is to show people and personalities. Exposures can be longer, of course, to allow the darker shadow areas to be clear, but this means the bright water becomes a 'burned-out', over-exposed area. There is no compromise. You have to decide the priority and expose accordingly. If left to auto-exposure, the dominant area will determine the exposure and if that is bright, the shadows will become obscure black areas.

Working from land, the distance from the subject is the greatest problem and the absence of powerful enough telephoto lenses limits possibilities. If using a zoom, then 200 mm is about the limit and most sailing must be relatively close. Longer – 300 mm, 400 mm – lenses are available at relatively modest cost, and converters which double the effective focal length can be

Sitting in a rescue boat at the leeward mark with an 80–200 mm zoom lens gives plenty of chances to take photos of the action.

added. The price to pay for a 2 times converter in terms of extra power is the loss of 2 f. stops on exposure and darkening of the viewfinder image which makes focusing harder. For any long telephoto lenses a tripod is essential.

500 mm mirror lenses are not too expensive and are light to handle. Although having a fixed f. stop they offer probably the best compromise.

On the Water
Unless spiritually endowed, you are going to need a power boat to provide a platform. To have any mobility it *must* be driven with consideration for all and any sailors. Primary considerations are: no interference if there is racing going on, and *no* hazard, with a clear look out at all times. You can circle around a race course and choose the shooting angle. Apply the same principles as from land. Any lens can be used and only the distance is your guiding factor. Remember again that the image in the viewfinder is true. Don't see it as you *want* to see it.

Best for exciting photos is to work with a friend sailing his board for the pictures. (They all love posing!) He can sail at, around or behind your boat.

Remember the hazards of salt water on your equipment. Wear an anorak which can cover your camera. Turn your back to the spray most of the time. At the end of the day, if spray has got at the gear, I always wipe it thoroughly with a wet, fresh water cloth and dry off as soon as I get back to base.

In the Water
No doubt you have looked at lots of sailboarding pictures and given some thought to how they were produced. Almost every time the

Shooting from the land gives a high vantage point when you use a long, tripod-mounted telephoto lens.

most exciting shots are made from an in-water position. Obviously, this calls for waterproof equipment so unless you have a waterproof housing for the normal SLR cameras it is necessary to have an actual waterproof camera. I use the long-established Nikonos, either the manual III or automatic V and prefer the control available on the older one. But apart from its bulk I would rather work with a proper waterproof housing which permits choice of lenses on the SLR camera, with a motor drive to ensure no good opportunities are missed. At the same time one must remember to conserve film – it can be a long swim and a hassle to get back ashore just to replace film.

Unless you are a good swimmer and feel totally at home in the water forget about this kind of windsurf photography. It's a waste of time if more effort goes into the swimming than the photography!

In Hawaii, the local surf photographers have the advantage of many years familiarity and experience against us very occasional in-water Europeans. And if the waves are difficult with coral near the surface one can feel very much a foreign body in the sea. In the UK and Europe of course, a full wet suit is generally necessary. Without waves a buoyancy aid gives helpful height in the water. Dive fins are almost a necessity for manoeuvrability.

Camera exposures are best set manually to suit the angle 'to sun you are choosing to shoot. A good spit on the protective glass now and again helps the salt water to slide off the lens protecting surface.

The services of a *competent, reliable* sailing subject are also a necessity. Remember it can be dangerous with a board tearing past (and hopefully not over) you.

Finally, remember that in the end it's not your equipment or the subject that makes the shot – it's how you shoot it.

Manufacturing Techniques

Most boards are made from an outer plastic skin completely filled with foam. This is usually polyurethane, mixed from two constituents which expand rapidly on contact.

The foam is injected after the skin has been made, and gives the board its shape, rigidity, and buoyancy. The distribution of the foam and its bond to the skin is critical. With enough hard use the foam in a badly made board will begin to separate, and will then start to break up.

A less usual alternative is polystyrene foam, which is lighter but weaker, and therefore generally requires a thicker skin. It is premoulded before being covered in the outer skin.

The three most popular skin materials are polyethylene, ABS/ASA and glassfibre.

Polyethylene

It is generally agreed that this is the toughest material, but there are problems. Tooling costs are high, and for some manufacturers it has taken several years to sort out an acceptable finish – they have been plagued by boards full of bumps, hollows, and weakness where the skin has run too thin.

It is easy to see whether a board has a 'fair' (ie smooth) finish, but not whether the polyethylene is thick enough in the right places, or indeed of the right quality.

There are two main methods of polyethylene manufacture: roto- and blow-moulding.

Roto-moulding

The Dutch windsurfer manufacturer Ten Cate is a leader in this field, and the way they roto-mould their boards is similar to techniques used by other manufacturers. The process starts with two sets of board-shaped metal moulds, which are mounted back to back. Each mould has a top and a bottom half, and the polyethylene powder is poured into the bottom half, before the top half is clamped on to it.

The moulds are then placed in a gas fired oven which heats them for around 20 minutes at 200°C. After the oven the moulds go to the cooler for a 15 minute blast of cold air. They are then opened, and the plastic skins literally ripped out by hand – they look rather like limp white sausages. The moulds then need minimal preparation with a release agent for the next cycle.

The plastic skins are placed in a foaming box – a metal mould which is the shape of the final board. Premeasured foam is shot in through a hole in the stern for around 30 seconds, and then left to expand and settle for 15 minutes. Any excess is normally allowed to escape – usually through the hole which will take the towing eye.

The board can then be removed from the foaming box. Excess polyethylene is trimmed by hand, and striping and detailing added before final packaging.

Blow-moulding

The number of blow-moulding plants is limited by their cost. One machine producing two boards at a time will cost around $250,000!

In this method the polyethylene is blown into the mould, rather as one would blow up a balloon. The theory is that this gives greater control over the spread of the thickness of the plastic.

ABS/ASA

ABS is a plastic material which is probably the most popular amongst board manufacturers.

It is not as tough a material as polyethylene, but it is easier for the manufacturer to get a good finish with it.

The process

There are various ways of producing an ABS board, and the French and German manufacturers have always been at the forefront of developments.

The first ABS boards were produced by heating a flat sheet of ABS, and then lowering it down so that it could envelop a metal mould. Like polyethylene, this led to problems with thinness and thickness. A better and more sophisticated technique has now been developed whereby the heated sheet is blown up on to the mould. The plastic skins forming the hull bottom and top are then taken from the moulds, and hand trimmed to remove the rough edges. The essential fittings (mast foot, daggerboard well, and skeg box units) are then bonded into place, before the two halves are joined.

The board is then placed in a foaming box, with the remainder of the process being similar to the finishing of polyethylene or glassfibre boards – it is only the skin material which is essentially different.

ABS/ASA + EPS

ASA is a variation on ABS which many German marques use in conjunction with EPS (polystyrene) to make high volume boards lighter. They use a rather different and highly sophisticated method of constructing their boards, which was first introduced in 1982.

They blow their polystyrene foam core first, and then mould the ASA around it compressing the whole lot together in a mould. The great advantage is that there is then no hull/deck join, as the skin is one continuous moulding without a break.

The problem is that polystyrene does not always bond well with ABS/ASA, and will be prone to delamination if put to very hard use. To overcome this, manufacturers have come up with the answer of putting an epoxy laminate of glassfibre (sometimes with Kevlar or carbon reinforcement) on the deck or all over between the polystyrene and ASA which makes a more successful bond. Mistral pioneered this technique with their *LCS* (Lightweight Compound Skin) system. Other leading manufacturers use similar techniques with similar fancy names and top-level price tags!

Glassfibre

Glassfibre is the most labour-intensive of the three materials. It is therefore the easiest to control, and has initial tooling costs which are a fraction of setting up polyethylene or ABS plants in both time and money. It is therefore favoured by the smaller manufacturers, and is more suitable for short-lived production runs of up-to-the-minute specialist boards which must be put into production quickly, and may be outdated in nine months. It is an ideal material for getting a good finish and controlling the weight, strengths, and weaknesses of a board, but as a shock absorbing skin it is far more fragile than the others.

The process

Glassfibre boards are made in moulds, similar to polyethylene or ABS, and the process is much the same as for yacht building.

The gel coat, which will become the shiny outer skin, is first sprayed or brushed into the mould – it is like a thick paint. Then the glass mat is laid in place, with extra thicknesses at the stress points, and the polyester resin is brushed in which turns it into hard glassfibre. Alternatively the glassfibre can be shot with a 'gun', that chops small strands of glass mat and sprays them at high speed on to the mould, together with a stream of resin.

In his search for strength with low weight, the builder can opt for:
1. Epoxy resin. Longer curing and more difficult to work with than polyester resin, but the same strength for less weight. It is usually used with polystyrene cores. Top class epoxy boards are made by 'compression forming', using vacuum and heat in a mould to ensure a very strong board.
2. Hollow boards. A hollow board

reinforced with ply 'stringers' and 'frames' will have great rigidity. Foam blocks must be inserted to provide buoyancy, but they have no structural value. Racing boards in Division II sometimes opt for this technique.

The main disadvantage of hollow boards is that they will be prone to leaks.
3. Foam sandwich. Usually used in conjunction with hollow boards.

A foam sandwich filling between the layers of glass mat gives the board an extra strong skin with little increase in weight. However, hard use can lead to delamination of the foam from the mat.
4. Exotic materials. Kevlar is stronger than glass mat, but more expensive and much more difficult to work with. Carbon fibre can be used as a strengthening material in places of stress, but has the same drawbacks.

Other Materials

Trade names

Trade names make the whole business of board construction somewhat confusing. *LCS*, *TDC*, *Copex* and *MDC* are just a few of the unusual names which will confront you. They can all be boiled down to the principal materials of polyethylene, ABS/ASA, and glassfibre.

Custom boards

Custom boards are hand-made, one-off boards. They have evolved from surfboard manufacture, and most of those sold worldwide are either made in Hawaii or the UK which are the main centres of custom construction.

The custom 'shaper' starts with a solid polystyrene or polyurethane foam core which is shaped like a box and about the size of the board. He cuts out the basic shape with a saw, and then uses grinding and sanding tools to perfect it. He then laminates the shaped core with glassfibre, puts in the fittings (such as skeg box, mast track and footstraps), and hey presto you have a

unique hand-made board.

Custom boards are normally bought by experts, and are mainly wave and strong wind boards of 2.80 m or less. They are light, stiff, but unfortunately very fragile; and are also notable for beautiful coloured airbrushing on both deck and bottom.

Wood

By definition wooden boards must be hand built.

A simple and cheap 'kit' method of construction is to make up a board with sheets of ply held together by glassfibre tape and copper wire 'stitches'. The disadvantages are that the ply sheets do not give much scope for shaping the board, which will be prone to leaks.

A far more complex alternative is to shape and glue thin sheets of ply laminate over a male mould. This is based on a classic method of dinghy construction, but has no conceivable advantages apart from producing a very beautiful board.

Manufacture of Fittings

Glassfibre masts are made up from pre-prepared glass and resin (usually epoxy) rolls, which are cut into mast-long lengths, and then wrapped around lightly heated stainless steel mandrils. These are placed in an oven for about 20 minutes, and the mast can then be slid off the mandril ready for use.

Alloy masts are made of tapered extrusions of aluminium. The wall thickness and diameter has a governing effect on the weight and bending characteristics of the mast.

Hull fittings

It is becoming increasingly common for all hull fittings and ancillaries – mast foot and well, skeg box, daggerboard case, daggerboard, skeg, towing eye, etc – to be manufactured by outside contractors. They are usually moulded in plastics such as ABS or polypropylene. The units are delivered ready to be bonded into the board.

Glossary

Note: Words in *italics* are explained elsewhere in the Glossary.

A

ABS
A plastic skin material used in the mass-production of boards.

Allround
An allround board is one that suits a wide variety of conditions. Usually this means that it is a *flatboard* or *allround-funboard* which is suitable for learners, more experienced sailors, and *strong wind* sailing.

Apparent wind
The wind that is experienced by the sailor – different in direction and speed from the *true wind* experienced by a stationary observer.

ASA
A skin material similar to *ABS*.

B

Bale out
There comes a time when you're jumping off a wave and feel that it's mutually beneficial if you and your board part company. Don't let it come back down on top of you.

Battens
Pieces of flexible *glass fibre* used to support the *roach* of the sail.

Bearing away
Sailing away from the wind – normally by inclining the *rig* forwards.

Beating
'Beating to *windward*' – sailing as close to the wind as possible.

Beaufort Scale
Admiral Beaufort invented the Beaufort Scale, a measurement of wind speed based on *knots*. The Beaufort Scale is measured from Force 0 to Force 12.

Blank
A foam blank is roughly board shape and size. It is 'shaped' into a *custom* board. The foam is either polyurethane (more usual) or polystyrene.

Boardsailing
How to avoid saying windsurfing.

Bow
The front end of the board.

Break
General surfing term for the wave and where it starts breaking. 'Shorebreak' is where it hits the shore.

C

Camber
The amount of curve in the sail – whether it is trimmed full or flat.

Carbon fibre
Strengthening material used in the construction of exotic boards.

Carve
To 'carve a *gybe*' or 'carve a turn' – altering course at high speed, achieved by pushing on the *rail* and banking the board like a ski.

Cavitation
The *skegs* and the back of the board cease to grip the water. The back of the board then slides away and *spins out*.

CE
The Centre of Effort – the fulcrum of the wind's power in the sail.

Chill factor
Getting cold due to the wind lowering your body temperature.

Chine
A flat surface, usually on the underside of the board.

Chord
An imaginary straight line drawn between the shortest distance from the *clew* of the sail to the *mast*.

Cleat
A small fitting used to secure a line. 'Clamcleats' are the popular sort, placed on the *wishbone* to secure the *outhaul* line.

Clew
The outer corner of the sail which is attached to the end of the *wishbone*.

Clew-first
To 'sail clew-first' – to sail with the *clew* pointing towards the wind. Used in *freestyle* and *strong wind* gybing techniques.

Close hauled
To sail as close to the wind as possible – beating, etc.

CLR
Centre of Lateral Resistance – the main point about which a board will resist and turn. In practice this usually means the *daggerboard*.

Custom
'Custom board' – hand made from a foam *blank*.

D

Dacron
A type of woven polyester fibre sailcloth.

Daggerboard
Large fin mid-way in the board, which is removable from the *daggerboard* case. Prevents the board going sideways.
  A *storm daggerboard* is much shorter, and makes the board easier to control beating in strong winds. Made in moulded plastic or laminated plywood.

Depression
Period of unsettled weather which normally means wind. Also called a *low*.

Displacement
'Displacement board' – loose term for board with rounded underwater shape to reduce *wetted area*. Usually refers to an *Open Class roundboard*.

Donkey kick
Kicking the back end of the board when you jump off a wave, so the board goes into vertical takeoff.

Donkey's ear
Strong wind *skeg*, shaped as above.

Downhaul line
Attaches the *tack* of the sail to the *universal joint*.

Drake
Jim Drake probably did most to invent windsurfing.

Dry suit
A neoprene suit, with neck and wrist seals, that keeps the water out. For cold weather windsurfing.

Duck tack
Ducking under the *rig*, rather than walking round the front of it. You can also 'duck *gybe*'.

E

Epoxy resin
Superior resin used to 'cure' glass mat, Kevlar, etc. Difficult to work with.

Eye of the wind
The precise direction from which the wind is blowing.

F

Fathead (Powerhead)
Strong wind sail with a full *head* supported by one or two *battens*. The theory is that you don't lose power down in the trough of waves, and can use a shorter *wishbone* for the same sail area. Most strong wind sails now use an elliptical shape supported by full length battens.

Fence
A fence or *cavitation* plate is a flat section like a small wing attached to a *skeg*. The theory is that it will disperse the passage of air bubbles which aerate the skeg and cause it to lose its grip on the water.

Fin
Another way of saying *skeg*. In strong wind terminology it could also refer to the *daggerboard*.

Floater
A board with enough buoyancy to carry your weight when stationary.

Foil
Like a V-shaped undercarriage. A hydrofoil will rise up and plane on its foil(s), requiring less power for more speed due to the diminished *wetted*

area. Not very successful in windsurfing applications.

Foot
The bottom of the sail.

Footstraps
Straps to put your feet in so you keep connected to the board.

Freestyle
Performing tricks on a board, which in a competition must normally be compressed into a three minute routine.

Full
A sail is trimmed 'full' or 'flat' depending on the amount of *camber*.

Funboard
Generally means a board that is fun to sail in stronger winds.

G

Gasket
A rubber or plastic strip which keeps the water out of the *daggerboard case* when the daggerboard is fully retracted into the *hull*.

Gate start
One board sails across the fleet on *port tack* as the start gun is fired. To start, all the other boards must sail behind its stern. Normally used when there is a big *one-design* fleet.

Glassfibre
Glass mat which is 'cured' with resin. Used to make production boards, *custom* boards, and *masts*. Also called GRP and fibreglass.

Gybing
Altering course so the stern passes through the *eye of the wind*.

H

Harness
Used so that you can 'hook in' to a harness line either side of the *wishbone*.

Head
Top of the sail.

Head up
Sail up towards the wind – usually by inclining the *rig* aft towards the stern.

High aspect ratio
A HAR sail is tall and narrow – a low aspect ratio sail is flat and squat.

Hot dogging
The forerunner of *freestyle*.

Hull
The basic board, excluding the *rig*.

Hypothermia
Losing body heat due to exposure. A very dangerous condition.

I

IBSA
International Boardsailing Association.

Inhaul
The inhaul line attaches the *wishbone* to the *mast*.

Ins-and-outs
Strong wind competition in which boards *reach* up and down a course.

IWS
International Windsurfing Schools.

IYRU
International Yacht Racing Union.

J

Jolly good time
What we have when the wind blows hard.

K

Kanger's cock
Obscene Australian vernacular referring to a *strong wind skeg* shaped as the above.

Kevlar
Vaguely 'exotic' material with stronger properties than glass mat. Tends to be much more expensive and is difficult to work with.

Knots
Nautical miles per hour. A nautical mile is 2000 yards (1.65 km) rather than the more familiar 1760.

L

Lamination
Sticking materials together. Glass mat is laminated with resin to make a board; sheet ply is laminated with glue to make a *daggerboard*.

Le Mans start
The racers stand at the water's edge. When the start gun goes they launch their boards, jump on, and sail off. Normally used to start a *long distance race* – it is spectacular to watch.

Leash
You must have a leash connecting the *rig* to the board in case the *mast foot* pulls out.

Leech
The edge of the sail between the *head* and the *clew*.

Leeward
The side of the board the wind is blowing to. Opposite to *windward*.

Leeway
'Making leeway' – the amount the board moves sideways, or to *leeward*.

Lifejacket
A lifejacket will float you face up, and help prevent you from drowning if you are knocked out. A 'buoyancy aid' will usually float you face down – most buoyancy in *harnesses* falls into this category.

Lip
The 'lip of the wave' – the crest when it's just breaking.

Long distance race
A 'marathon' over at least 10 miles, hopefully more like 25 miles. Organizers try to include long reaching legs.

Long John
The popular windsurfing *wetsuit* – one-piece with long legs and no arms. You can wear a 'bolero' jacket on top.

Low
A *depression* – unsettled weather and wind.

Luff
The edge of the sail from the *head* to the *tack*. Next to the 'luff sleeve'.

Luff perpendicular
The measurement between the *wishbone* slot and the *clew*. Used by sailmakers.

Luffing
Heading up into the wind; heading up so that the wind strikes the *leeward* side of the sail; letting out the sail so that the wind does likewise. To 'luff a competitor' is to head up and force him to sail higher than he wishes to during a race.

M

Marginal sail
A sail for use when it's blowing too hard for a full size *regatta* sail. Normally around 5.0 square metres depending on conditions.

Mast
Either made out of *glassfibre* or alloy – usually of uniform length.

Mast foot
Fits into the mast foot well or track, and is normally permanently attached to the *universal joint*. Every manufacturer seems to have a different fitting.

Maxi
A sail of 7 square metres or more, used for light conditions.

Munched
Eg 'He was munched by a wave'.

Mylar
Sailcloth made from a polyester film which sandwiches a 'scrim' or Dacron.

N

Neoprene
Fabric used for *wetsuits*, boots, gloves, etc. If it's unlined it's warmer (on the water off a duck's back principle) but prone to tearing.

Non-slip
Most boards have non-slip finishes moulded into the deck surface. They vary considerably, and can be improved by non-slip paint, or board *wax*.

Nose
Front end, or *bow* of the board.

O

Offshore wind
Wind blowing away from the shore.

Olympic triangle
The IYRU race course for boards, with three equal legs and 60 degree turns at each mark. Normal length of each leg is around one mile for an international event. The fleet usually sails round the triangle, followed by a 'sausage' leaving out the wing mark.

One-design
A class of identical boards – eg the *Windsurfer* Regatta.

Onshore wind
Wind blowing on to the shore.

Open class
Different boards racing together to the same design and construction rules. Open Class Division 1 is for flatboards; Open Class Division 2 is for roundboards.

Outhaul
Line to pull the *clew* of the sail out to the end of the *wishbone*.

P

Patent
Hoyle *Schweitzer* patented the concept of the *windsurfer*, and has chased his adversaries through the courts ever since.

Pentathlon
A *regatta* where five events count towards an overall prize; such as triangle racing, *long distance race*, *freestyle*, *slalom*, and *ins-and-outs*.

Pintail
A board designed for *strong winds* with a tapering *stern* for better control.

Plane
To skim across the water, rather than sailing through it.

Polyethylene
Plastic skin material used to mass produce boards. Always used with polyurethane.

Polystyrene/polyurethane
Two types of foam used for providing the solid filling of boards.

Pop-out
A mass production board. It 'pops-out' of a mould.

Port
Left (looking forward). Indicated by the colour red.

Purling
Sticking the nose of the board into the wave and invariably going head over heels.

Pumping
Pumping the rig back and forth creates wind in the sail and gives the board a lot of extra speed. However in IYRU racing you are only allowed 'three pumps to promote planing' – deciding who is and who isn't within the rules leads to a lot of protests and bad feeling.

Q

QED
A *radical freestyle* demonstration.

R

Radical
US windsurfing expression ('I was putting in some really radical jumps – was I 50 or 60 feet clear?')

Rail
The side of the board. 'Riding the rail' is standing on the side.

Railing
Sailing along, with the board slightly on its side, induced by the push of the *mast foot* and the aquaplaning effect of the *daggerboard*. This technique is positively encouraged by sailors on upwind legs, as it reduces the *wetted area* of the board.

Reaching
Sailing with the wind on the beam – ie with the wind at or near 90 degrees to the board's course. You can sail a close reach, a beam reach, and a broad reach.

Regatta
A meeting with a series of races. A 'regatta sail' is a loose description of a sail which fits within the *Open Class* regatta norm – eg around 6.3 sq m.

Resin
Turns glass mat into *glassfibre*.

Rig
Everything above the level of the *universal joint* (*mast*, sail, *wishbone* etc.)

Roach
The area of the sail which is supported by the *battens* – eg anything outside a straight line from the *head* to the *clew*.

Rocker
Curvature in the fore and aft plane of a board – a board that is absolutely flat underneath has no rocker (or 'scoop').

Roto-moulding
A method of moulding *polyethylene* boards, by rotating and rocking the moulds.

Roundboard
A racing board with an underwater profile that is round, and therefore cuts down *wetted area*, but is unstable. Normally refers to an *Open Class* Division 2 board.

Running
Sailing with the wind directly, or almost directly behind.

S

Sandwich
'Foam sandwich construction' has a skin made of two very thin skins (*glassfibre* or *Kevlar*) sandwiching a layer of foam around 1 cm thick. The board will normally be hollow, and this construction method enables it to be very strong and light.

Schweitzer
Hoyle Schweitzer helped invent the windsurfer with Jim *Drake*. He then patented it.

Scoop
Rocker at the nose of the board.

Set
Two waves, from crest to crest, travelling together.

Shaper
A person who shapes a foam *blank* into a board. He uses a saw, a plane, and a sanding tool.

Shims
Friction pads to ensure the *daggerboard* fits tightly in its case.

Shockcord
Elasticated cord that prevents the sailor losing the *uphaul*.

Simulator
A shore-bound *windsurfer* mounted on a turntable. Used for teaching by the *IWS* system.

Sinker
A board that sinks beneath you when stationary.

Skeg
Small fin at the *stern* of a board, to keep it sailing straight.

Slalom
A *regatta* knock-out competition in which two competitors *gybe* and *tack* round a small course.

Slot rubber
As with *gasket*. Keeps the water out of the *daggerboard* case when the daggerboard is retracted into the *hull*.

Speed trial
The fastest board over 500 metres during a timed run.

Spin-out
See *cavitation*.

Spreader bar
An aluminium bar which you wear across your chest to spread the load of the *harness*.

Starboard
Right (looking forward). Indicated by the colour green.

Stern
Back end of the board.

Storm daggerboard
A short *daggerboard*.

Strong wind board
As for *funboard* – a board specifically for *strong winds*, normally with *footstraps*, low volume, etc.

T

Tack
See Tacking. Alternatively the corner of the sail down by the *universal joint*.

Tacking
Altering course so the *nose* of the board passes through the *eye of the wind*. You do this if you want to sail towards the direction the wind is coming from. Could be called 'going about'.

Tail
Back end of the board.

Tandem
A *windsurfer* made for two.

Terylene
The type of woven polyester material they make many sails from. Similar to Dacron.

Tide
Coastal movement of the sea induced by pull of the sun and the moon. Tidal rip is when it runs extremely fast around a headland or in a confined area – it should be treated with respect by any sensible *windsurfer*.

Towing eye
In the *nose* of the board. To take a towing line, should you wish to be taken in tow.

Trim
To 'trim the sail' – letting it in and out as the wind changes.

True wind
The wind that is experienced by a stationary observer – different from the *apparent wind* experienced by someone on the move.

Tube
When a wave breaks on rapidly shelving ground, it creates a tube as the top curls over. The surfers travel along it.

U

Universal joint
Normally attached permanently to the *mast foot*, the UJ allows the *rig* to be swung through 360 degrees and inclined through a minimum of 180 degrees. The mast foot/universal joint unit is the adaptor between the rig and the board.

Uphaul
The rope used to pull the rig out of the water. It is attached to the *UJ* by *shockcord* – an alternative arrangement is an elasticated 'Hawaiian uphaul'.

V

Volume
The volume of the board determines its buoyancy, and to some extent its speed. If you weigh 300 pounds, make sure that you don't get a board that sinks under you.

W

Waterstart
Starting sailing when you're lying in the water, with the *rig* on top of you to *windward* of the board. Much used in *freestyle* and *de rigueur* for *sinkers* – it's not as easy as it might look.

Wax
Non-slip wax to help you stand on your board. ('Sex Wax' is a top selling brand.)

Weight groups
Division of competitors by weight for *triangle racing*. There are liable to be a maximum of four categories.

Wetted area
The area of the board that's in contact with the water. The less wetted area, the less drag, and the faster the board will go.

Windshift
A sudden shift in the wind's direction. When racing on upwind legs, competitors always *tack* on a windshift – it's the basis of tactics.

Windsurfer
Windsurfer with a capital W is a trade name – the original windsurfer invented by Hoyle *Schweitzer*. That's why some people talk about 'sailboards' and 'board sailing', rather than windsurfers and windsurfing.

Windward
The side of the board the wind is blowing from. Opposite to *leeward*.

Wipe-out
Taking an almighty fall.

Wishbone
The booms, made from two elliptical alloy tubes with plastic/nylon end fittings.

Appendices

Windsurfing Magazines

UK
On Board
Boardsailing International Ltd
28 Parkside
Wollaton
Nottingham.
Tel: 0602 226798

Windsurf
Ocean Publications Ltd
34 Buckingham Palace Rd
London SW1.
Tel: 01–828 4551

Surf News
PO Box 1
Hayling Island
Hampshire.

France
Planche
51 bis, Route de la Reine
92100 Boulogne/Billancourt

Planche No 1
75 Rue D'Amsterdam
75008 Paris.

Planche à Voile
15 Rue d'Argenteuil
75001 Paris.

Wind
28 Rue des Petites-Ecuries
75010 Paris.

Germany
Surf
Sachsenkamstrasse 19
Postfach 801008
8000 München 70.

Surf Journal
Ortlerster 8
8000 München 70.

Windsurfing Magazine
Ferdinand Maria Str 30
8000 München 19.

Netherlands
Surfsport
Z HD Hernn Paul Knopp
Postbus 50057
Netherlands 1305 AB Almere.

Surf Magazine
Z HD Herrn Van Wagensveld
Postbus 264
Netherlands 4200 Gorinchen.

Windsurfer
Herrn W Koesen
Herengracht 566
Amsterdam.

De Windsurfer
Z HD Hernn G Cooreman
Oosterdstraat 13
Netherlands 9000 Gent.

Japan
Hi Wind
Marine Planning Co Ltd
7F NS Building
2–2–3 Sarugaku-cho
Chiyoda-ku
Tokyo.

Austria
Ossterr Windsurfing Revue
Schidbaucr
Schwarzenbergplatz 10
A-1040 Wien.

Sweden
Windsurfing
La Dore 65
Box 25033
10023 Stockholm.

USA
Windsurf
1955 W 190th St
Torrance
Ca 90509

Sailboarder
PO Box 1028
Dana Point
Ca 92629.

Board & Sail
PO Box 8108
Sacramento
Ca 95818.

Boardsailor
20 E Palm Avenue
Nokomis
Florida 33555.

Windsurfing Addresses

1. International Bodies
IYRU
60 Knightsbridge, London SW1.
Tel: 01–235 6221
The International Yacht Racing Union is the backbone of yacht racing throughout the world. With a few exceptions such as professional racing, most windsurfer races are run to IYRU rules.

IBSA
55 Avenue Kléber
75784 Paris Cedex 16
France.
Tel: 01 553 68 00.
The International Boardsailing Association founded the Open Class, doing all the initial development work on what is now Division 2. They have run the World and European championships for this class, but suffered a reversal in financial fortunes in 1982.

2. International Class Associations
IWCA
The Secretary
1955 West 190th St
Torrance Ca 90509
USA.
Tel: 213 515 4900.
The International Windsurfer Class Association has the greatest number of members who race one-design. Its World, European, and National championships are always extremely popular.

IWGCA
The Secretary
17/18 Sherman Avenue
Evanston
Illinois 60201
USA.
Tel: 312 475 3381.
The International Windglider Class is the only one-design association with membership behind the Iron Curtain, and was the IYRU's Olympic choice for 1984.

IMCO
Kerzer Sgracht 506
1017 E7
Amsterdam
Netherlands.
Tel: 2024 8961
The International Mistral Class Association (Mistral Light) is the youngest of the three international one-design associations.

3. International Regatta Organizers

Kailua Bay Windsurfing Association
PO Box 1224
Kailua
Hawaii 9 68 34.
Organizers of the famous Pan Am Cup. It's held each year in late March, but you should get your entry form the previous autumn.

Euro-Funboard Cup
Beethovenstrasse 10
8000 Munich 2
W. Germany.
The Euro-Funboard Cup is the major European strong wind series, with categories for both professional and amateur. It is run by Peter Brockhaus, a father figure of the Pan Am Cup.

WSP
30 Rochester Square
London NW1.
Windsurfing Professional organizes professional regattas which are run to its own racing rules. It tends to favour multi-discipline events.

4. UK National Bodies

RYA
Victoria Way
Woking Surrey.
Tel: 048 62 5022.
The Royal Yachting Association acts as the governing body of yachting in the UK, and is primarily involved with windsurfing's teaching aspects.

UKBSA
30 Rochester Square
London NW1.
Tel: 01–267 3686.
The United Kingdom Boardsailing Association is the biggest windsurfing association in the UK. It is heavily involved in Division 1 and 2 Open Class racing.

Scottish Boardsailing Association
Clearview
Argyll Street
Lochgilpead
Argyll
An association with aims allied to the UKBSA.

5. UK Windsurfing Schools

IWS
Unit 10
Stort Valley Industrial Park
Bishops Stortford
Herts.
Tel: 0279 53456.
The English branch of International Windsurfer Schools which evolved and developed the mode of teaching favoured throughout the world for the past decade.

RYA
Victoria Way
Woking
Surrey.
Tel: 048 62 5022.
The RYA uses the IWS system for its recognized windsurfing schools throughout the UK.

6. UK Class Associations

Dufour Wing
25 Dearne Croft
Deighton Bar
Wetherby
West Yorkshire.
Tel: 0937 64462.

Jet
Ryetop
Matts Hill Rd
Hartlie
Sittingbourne
Kent.
Tel: 0634 361414.

Laser Surfsprint
5 Ryden Avenue
Kingsteignton
Newton Abbot
South Devon.
Tel: 0626 5734.

Sailboard
41 Brent Rd
Tinkers Bridge
Milton Keynes.
Tel: 0908 676689.

Sea Panther
11 Dagmar Grove
Beeston
Nottingham.
Tel: 0602 227037

Windglider
55 Victoria Rd
Ellacombe
Torquay
Devon.
Tel: 0803 212411.

Windsurfer
21 Brook Gardens
Emsworth
Hampshire.
Tel: 024 34 6265.

Mistral
Kent College
Canterbury
Kent.
Tel: 0424 441189.

Specialist Windsurfing Bibliography

The Rules Book Eric Twiname (Granada) £3.95.
Paul Elvstrom Explains the Yacht Racing Rules Paul Elvstrom (Creagh-Osborne & Partners) £4.25
Two small books that explain the IYRU yacht racing rules clearly and concisely. Very useful to anyone who wants to go windsurfer racing.

Sailboard Racing Rainer Gutjahr (Macmillan) £7.95
A book which is specifically dedicated to racing a board round an Olympic triangle – useful for those requiring more information.

Instant Weather Forecasting Alan Watts (Granada) £3.50
An excellent little book that explains the basics of understanding the weather, and shows you how to forecast the wind and weather by keeping an eye on the sky.

Meteorology At Sea Ray Sanderson (Stanford Maritime) £8.85
Considerably more complex and really intended for the yachtsman, but interesting for the windsurfer who would like to know more.

Windsurfing Results

Open Class Division 2 World Championship

1979 Guadeloupe.
Lightweight: Karl Messmer/Switzerland/Mistral.
Ladies: Marie Anick Maus/France/Tornado.

1980, Israel.
Lightweight: Karl Messmer/Switzerland/Mistral.
Heavyweight: Thomas Staltmaier/W. Germany/Mistral.
Ladies: Manuelle Graveline/France/Dufour.

1981, St. Petersburg, USA.
Lightweight: Stephan van der Berg/Netherlands/Tornado.
Heavyweight: Jan Wangaard/Norway/Sailboard.
Ladies: Maren Berner/Norway/Sailboard.

Windsurfing Results after 1981

Open Class Division 2 World Championship

1982, Guadeloupe
Lightweight: Robert Nagy/France/Crit.
Heavyweight: Gildas Guillerot/France/Crit.
Ladies: Marie Annick Maus/France.

1983, Spain
Lightweight: Robert Nagy/France/Crit.
Heavyweight: Gildas Guillerot/France/Crit.
Ladies: Manuelle Graveline/France/Dobbelmann.

1984, Kenya
Lightweight: Robert Nagy/France/Crit.
Heavyweight: Anders Bringdal/Sweden/Lechner.
Ladies: Manuelle Graveline/France/Tiga.

1985, UK
Lightweight: Hervé Piegelin/France/Profil.
Heavyweight: Jonas Davidson/Sweden/Davidson.
Ladies: Valerie Salles/France/Crit.

World Cup

1983
1. Robbie Naish/USA/Mistral & Gaastra
2. Ken Winner/USA/Bic & Pryde
3. Alex Aguera/USA/Mistral & Gaastra

1984
1. Robbie Naish/USA/Nistral & Gaastra
2. Ken Winner/USA/Bic & North
3. Robert Teriitehau/France/Browning & Gaastra

1985
1. Robbie Naish/USA/Mistral & Gaastra
2. Alex Aguera/USA/Tiga & Neil Pryde
3. Raphael Salles/France/Tiga & Gaastra

World Speed Record

1982
27.82 knots: Pascal Maka/France/Sailboard Maui-Ellesse.

1983
30.82 knots: Fred Haywood/USA/Sailboards Maui & Pryde.

1984
No record.

1985
32.35 knots: Michael Pucher/Austria/Five Star.

Sailcloth Brand Names

The proliferation of brand names and trade marks used in sails is confusing, but can be boild down to three basic forms and four basic materials.
The basic forms are:
Woven fabric
Film
Laminate of film and woven fabric
The basic materials are:
Nylon
Polyester
PVC
Aramatic polymides
The list which follows includes most of the brand names and generic terms used by windsurfer sailmakers.

Air Force
English supplier of 3 ply laminate consisting of a very open scrim sandwiched between two layers of polyester film.

Aquaflite
Dutch sailcloth supplier.

Aqualam
Trade name used by GTS to describe their large range of laminate sail fabrics.

Cordura
Trade name of heavy duty nylon used on luff tubes.

CYT
Condition Yarn Tempered hard resin finish, developed by Howe & Bainbridge.

Dacron
Dupont's trade name for their polyester fibre.

'Duo film'
Term used to describe a film/scrim/film laminate.

Dupont
American chemical company.

GTS
UK based producer of sail laminates.

Howe & Bainbridge
Dutch/American fabric supplier.

ICI
UK based chemical company producing polyester in film and fabric form.

Kevlar
Aramatic polymide produced by Dupont with very low stretch characteristic.

Laminar
Hood Sails' name for their polyester film.

Laminar Kevlar
Polyester film/aramatic polymide laminate.

LDS
Low Diagonal Stretch hard resin finish developed by Ten Cate of Holland.

Melinex
ICI's polyester film.

'Mono film'
Polyester film.

Mylar
Dupont's polyester film.

Plasti Pane.
PVC window material.

Polyant
German cloth producer.

Porcher Marine
French cloth producer.

Rip Stop Mylar
F2's 3 ply polyester with rip stop pattern. Made by Polyant.

'Scrim'
Loosely woven polyester cloth.

Sealam
Name used by Porcher Marine to describe their range of laminated fabrics.

Surfkote
Name used by Howe & Bainbridge to describe their Taffeta laminate.

'Taffeta'
A type of laminate consisting of one layer of polyester film bonded to a light closely woven fabric (one sided).

Tejin
Japanese sailcloth producer.

Tejin film
Japanese made polyester film.

Ten Cate
Dutch sailcloth producer.

Terylene
ICI's polyester fibre.

Tetron
Japanese polyester fibre.

Tri Lam
Trade name used by GTS to describe 3 ply (film/scrim/film) laminates.

'Warp strong'
Material designed with less stretch in the warp (along the roll).

'Weft Strong'
Material designed with less stretch in the weft (across the roll).

7. U.S. Windsurfing Associations

Board Sailing USA
Brian Tulley, Director
Box 2157
Citrus Heights, California 95611
This association of boardsailors and operators runs a program of boardsailing fleets throughout the nation.

International Windsurfer Class Association
Kathy Truax, Coordinator
1955 West 190th Street
P.O. Box 2950
Torrence, California 90509

The 18 districts of the IWCA cover the entire continental U.S. as well as Puerto Rico, the Virgin Islands, Mexico, Canada, Argentina and Columbia. You can get the phone numbers and addresses of the district captain in your area by writing to the above address.

8. U.S. Windsurfing Schools

Boardsailing Instructor's Group
c/o Susan Allen
4935 Sunshine Lane
Sacremento, California 95841

International Windsurfer Sailing Schools
Michael Ross
1955 West 190th Street
Torrence, California 90509
Both of these groups conduct schools throughout the nation. Write for information and addresses of schools in your area.

Specialist Windsurfing Bibliography

American Practical Navigator, available through the Superintendent of Documents, U.S. Government Printing Office, Washington D.C. 02402.
Includes information on weather, navigation, as well as many charts.

The Rules Book, Eric Twiname (Scribner's) $5.95
Paul Elvstrom Explains the Yacht Racing Rules, Ed. by Richard Creagh-Osborne (De Graff) $6.50
Two small books that explain IYRU yacht racing rules clearly and concisely. Very useful to anyone who wants to go windsurfer racing.

Tactics and Strategy in Yacht Racing, Joachim Schult (Dodd, Mead & Co., Inc).
A great introduction to racing tactics.

Sailboarding: A Beginner's Guide to Boardboat Sailing, A. H. Drummond, Jr. (Doubleday) $4.95

Sailboarding, Peter Brockhaus and Ulrich Stanciu (Mayflower) $8.95

Windsurfer World Championship

1975, France
Light: Matt Schweitzer/USA.
Medium Light: Brian Tulley/USA.
Medium Heavy: Derk Thijs/Netherlands.
Heavy: Helgo Zarges/W. Germany.
Ladies: Susie Swatek/USA.

1976, Bahamas
Light: Robbie Naish/USA.
Medium Light: M. Garaudée/France.
Medium Heavy: Derk Thijs/Netherlands.
Heavy: KH Stickl/W. Germany.
Ladies: Susie Swatek/USA.

1977, Sardinia
Light: Robbie Naish/USA.
Medium Light: Nino Stickl/W. Germany.
Medium Heavy: Guy Ducrot/France.
Heavy: Anders Foyen/Norway.
Ladies: Claudine Forest-Fourcade/France.

1978, Mexico
Light: Robbie Naish/USA.
Medium Light: Matt Schweitzer/USA.
Medium Heavy: Anders Foyen/Norway.
Heavy: Johnny Myrin/Sweden.
Ladies: Bev Thijs/Netherlands.

1979, Greece
Light: Marc Nieuwborg/France.
Medium Light: Thierry Eude/France.
Medium Heavy: J. Salen/Sweden.
Heavy: Cort Larned/USA.
Ladies: Manuelle Graveline/France.

1980, Bahamas
Light: Karl Messmer/Switzerland.
Medium Light: Frederic Gautier/France.
Medium Heavy: Thomas Staltmaier/W. Germany.
Heavy: G. Long/USA.
Ladies: Manuela Maschia/Italy.

1981, Japan
Light: Mike Waltze/USA.
Medium Light: Robert Nagy/France.
Medium Heavy: Frederick Gautier/France.
Heavy: Johnny Myrin/Sweden.
Ladies: Manuela Maschia/Italy.

Pan Am Cup

1980
Robbie Naish/USA/Mistral Naish.

1981
Ken Winner/USA/Dufour.

1982
Robbie Naish/USA/Mistral Naish.

World Speed Record

1977
17.1 knots: Derk Thijs/Netherlands/lightweight Windglider.

1979
19.2 knots: Clive Colenso/UK/Olympic Gold.

1980
24.45 knots: Jaap van der Rest/Netherlands/TC Special.

1982
27.82 knots: Pascal Maka/France/Sailboard Maui-Ellesse.

The Open Class

Divisions 1 and 2
Divisions 1 and 2 (flatboard and roundboard) have virtually the same measurement specifications, with the major exception of the depth of board: Division 1 is not more than 16.5 cm; Division 2 is not more than 22 cm.
The full Division 1 and 2 rules can be obtained from the IYRU. They can be summarised as follows:
Overall length: 3920 cm max.
Beam at widest point: 630 mm min.
Other beam restrictions: Not less than 590 mm for lengths of 1300 mm.
Depth of board: not more than 165 mm.
Division 1: Not more than 220 cm.
Division 2: Weight of board: 18 kg min.
Daggerboard: 700 cm max depth from underside of board.
Skeg: 300 mm max.
Mast: 4700 mm max.
Buoyancy: The Division 2 board shall either have three watertight compartments dividing its total volume into approximately equal parts, or a minimum of 0.1 cubic metres of rigid closed cell foam. The Division 1 board shall be entirely filled with rigid closed cell plastic foam of approved density.
Safety: A towing eye and mast leash must be fitted. There shall be no sharp upward projecting edges of radius less than 15 mm.
Materials: High modulus fibres such as Kevlar are prohibited.
Footstraps: Prohibited.
Limitation of equipment: During a race meeting only one board, two sails, and two daggerboard may be used. The board shall not be altered in any way during the race meeting.
Harness: Permitted.
Compass: Prohibited.
Weight Groups: Two are recommended, up to and over 70 or 75 kg.

Division 1 and 2 Sails
Division 1 and 2 sails have the same specifications and are interchangeable:

Luff	4400 mm
Leech	4300
Head to mid foot	4300
¾ height width	940
½ height width	1680
¼ height width	2270
Foot	2580

Division 1 Homologation
Division 2 is open to any one-off prototype, or production board that satisfies the measurement rules.
Division 1 is restricted to:
A. An IYRU International Class ie. Windsurfer, Windglider, Mistral.
B. A class approved by the IYRU of which there are not less than 2000 similar boards satisfying the measurement rules. NB. When Division 1 was introduced into the UK in 1982, no clas es (apart from the three International Cl .ses) satisfied B. Therefore the RYA held 'flatboard trials' and homologated the following boards: Alpha Waikiki, Beacher, Comet, Dufour Wind, Hunter, Hi Fly 555, Icarus, Jet Surf, Klepper S3, Magnum 370, Mirage Aloha, Mistral Kailua, Mistral Naish, Rcix 390, Rocker Regatta, Sailboard Carib, Sailboard Delta, Sailboard Grand Prix, Sailboard Sport, Sailboard Vario, Sea Panther, Yess.

Division 3
Open Class Division 3 covers tandems. The measurement specifications and class rules are similar to Division 2, with the very obvious exception that Division 3 allows two rigs and two drivers! There are also the following main differences:
Overall length: 6800 mm max.
Beam at widest point: Not less than 650 mm/not more than 750 mm.
Depth of board: Not more than 250 mm.
Weight of board: 50 kg min.
Daggerboard: 910 cm max depth from underside of board.

Windsurfing Racing
International Yacht Racing Union Rules
The IYRU rules are complex and lengthy enough to need a book to themselves. Either of the two books suggested in the Windsurfing Bibliography are strongly recommended if you intend racing.

The rules for boards are the same as those used for yachts and dinghies with a few exceptions. This is not always ideal, as a windsurfer is very different from other sail craft, and in some cases regatta organisers such as WSP have drafted their own very much more simple rules to be used during their own events.

Index

Acknowledgements

Jeremy Evans would like to thank the following who have all helped in one way or another with this book: Will Sutherland; Peter Williams of Hayling Windsurfing and Chelsea Wharf Windsurfing; Dee Caldwell of Dee Caldwell's Sailboard Centre; Mike Lingwood of Surf Sales Ltd.; James and Jane Ellis of Poole Windsurfing Centre; and Pan Am for laying on windsurfing in Hawaii.

Thanks to Philip Clark and Julian Holland who made the book possible; and finally thanks to Lesley who was the most help of all.

Photo Credits
Where not otherwise credited, photographs are by Alastair Black. Photographs from other sources appear on the following pages:
Chelsea Wharf Windsurfing: 38–39
Jeremy Evans: 43, 84, 86–87, 91, 107, 104
Fanatic: 89
Hayling Windsurfing: 37
Andrew Hooper: 113
Klepper: 83
Roger Lean-Vercoe: 31, 131
Mistral: 6–7, 15, 16, 20 (below), 22, 76, 107 (below)
Christian Petit: 127
Neil Pryde: 128
Sodim: 150, 151, 152, 153, 154, 155
Tabur: 157
Cliff Webb: 24, 25, 31, 35, 37, 44, 63, 73, 126, 128 (below), 129, 130, 131, 132, 133, 137, 139, 140, 142, 145, 147, 148
Alex Williams: Front cover, 17, 27, 29, 59, 75, 125